DEFIANT
POLITICAL
OPPRESSORS

★ **INVITE A** ★

DIVINE
JUDGMENT

**When Ol' Pharaoh and His Army
Just Won't Let the Nation Go Free**

Rev. Dr. Walter Arthur McCray
Gospelizer

SMALL BOOKS **BIG IDEAS**

Defiant Political Oppressors Invite a Divine Judgment
When Ol' Pharaoh and his army just won't let the nation go free

By Rev. Dr. Walter Arthur McCray, *Gospelizer*

P.O. Box 5369 • Chicago, IL 60680
Ph. 773.826.7790 • Fax 773.826.7792
Email: info@blacklightfellowship.com
https://www.BlackLightFellowship.com

ISBN: 978-0-933176-32-4

First Edition, 2021.

Editorial Services: Mary C. Lewis, MCL Editing, Etc.,
Evanston, IL   **mclwriter@msn.com**

Cover Services: Michelle D. Muhammad, MDM Design,
Chicago, IL   **mdm_621@yahoo.com**

To those who

dare to embrace the efficacy of

a present-day divine retribution

to preserve a democratic America—

true, just, and free.

Contents

DEFIANT POLITICAL OPPRESSORS

INVITE A

DIVINE JUDGMENT

1

SOCIAL-POLITICAL CRISES, CONSEQUENCES, AND THEOLOGICAL PERSPECTIVE

Time has well arrived for making a theological review of the nation's political-social state. The moment is crucial. We must recall those events and situations that have brought our nation to its critical hour of crises. Connecting the political-social dots with a theological perspective is the task. An honest and insightful analysis should give us a better understanding of our national sickness, and its after-effects. It will also indicate the adversity and suffering that we can expect will result if the hostile political temper of

Trump and his Trumpism prevails in the nation, and God intervenes with a judgment.

Converging Crises in 2020/21

What were the key events that brought the nation to a tipping point, even to our knees? How did this downward spiral so quickly come upon the nation? Consider what has happened.

Tumultuous events that took place in the election season rocked the nation to its core. Starting early in 2020 and continuing into 2021, the nation wrestled with social-political crises for an extended season. During this period, America came face-to-face with the converging crises of COVID-19, of economic stress, of racial unrest and reckoning, and of political divisiveness. Everything greatly intensified with the brutal public murder in May 2020 of George Floyd by law enforcement officers. Protests for Black racial justice, focusing on the racially evocative murders of Floyd, Breonna Taylor, and Ahmaud Arbery sprang up throughout the nation.[1] The extremely infectious coronavirus spread rapidly, and its financial consequences of shutdowns and layoffs forced the nation's economy into the tank, despite the growth of the stock market.

---

[1] A white police officer who pressed his knee on George Floyd's neck for 8 minutes and 46 seconds publicly murdered him in Minneapolis, MN. Plainclothes white police officers firing a hail of bullets terminated the life of Breonna Taylor on a midnight forced-entry raid into her apartment in Louisville, KY. White men near Brunswick in Glynn County, GA, murdered Ahmaud Arbery by pursuing and fatally shooting the innocent jogger. Issues of police brutality and misconduct, and racial injustice against Blacks were prevalent in these cases.

In 2020/21, our nation was passing through uncharted, troubling social-political waters. Moreover, the hotly contested presidential campaign exacerbated the crises, and then became a political crisis within itself.

Trumpism and Defiant Political Oppressors

◊ Trump's Trumpism — An Evil Crisis

Ex-president Trump is best known for "Trumpism," the very destructive ideology of its namesake. Trump—his campaign, startling election, and governing style—became the poster child of "Trumpism," his movement to "make America great again." Most of its negative characteristics were already present in the history of the nation; however, Trump provoked and instigated them with a vengeance. The ideas and actions of this ideology, that centers itself in white racism and supremacy, flies directly in the face of the nation's best ideals. It also dashes the hopes of millions of diverse Black and other peoples of color in the nation, and across the globe too.

Trumpism became entrenched in the lives and ethos of millions of whites, especially white Evangelicals. Their newfound "savior" authentically represented their political-religious base, and arguably their **basest** values. Trump's Trumpism crystallized a way of viewing and living the American life that is adhered to by an overwhelming number of the nation's white citizens.

"Trumpism" is a spirit—an evil spirit. The spirit of Trumpism ideology manifests itself in ungodly words, attitudes, actions, and policies—in a "wisdom" that is not from above, but in an anti-spiritual mentality that is "**earthly, sensual, and devilish.**"[2]

Among many other negative traits and political practices, the following characteristics of "Trumpism" are apparent: lies and deceptions; *hubris*, arrogance; biblical, historical ignorance; racism, white supremacy, white nationalism; divisive, incendiary rhetoric and practices; misogyny; partiality to the rich; immigrant insensitivity; anti-media bias; and refusal to repent.[3]

Trumpism is worse.

◊ Defiant Oppression —
An Extreme Crisis and Attempted Coup

Extreme political divisiveness characterized the nation's politics during the Trump administration. This was the nation's initial political crisis of 2020.[4] Making matters worse, the obstructionist actions of the defeated president and his operatives became **hostile and persecutory.** Ex-president Trump and his political enforcers were able to morph the nation's divisiveness into a crisis of **defiant political**

---

[2] See James 3:15.

[3] Rev. Dr. Walter Arthur McCray, "'Trumpism' Opposed by Evangelical Black Values," NBEA, 2018. https://www.the-nbea.org/wp-content/uploads/2018/11/Trumpism-Opposed-by-Black-Evangelical-Values-Rev.-Dr.-McCray-M.png

[4] Periodically, similar political-social crises have gripped the nation. Some include the race riots of the 1960s; the "Red Summer" of lynchings in 1919; the shutdown of Reconstruction; the Nullification crisis during the presidency of Andrew Jackson, etc.

oppression. Their actions demonstrate a perpetration of oppression—political and otherwise.

Ex-president Trump and his enforcers clearly revealed their persistently oppressive and subversive nature, and the presidential campaign and 2020 election magnified this situation. Trump and his followers defiantly refused to cut their election losses and move their hindering presence out of the way, to free the nation from their terrorizing tactics. Instead, they have pursued/persecuted their political opposites— those persons and groups who sought freedom and justice through their resistance, social activism, and historic vote.

The defeated ex- and his operatives forced their persecution to mutate. They transformed their political oppression into an attack on the governing system of **American democracy**; they calculatedly fought against the essence of the nation's commonly shared **historic democratic values**.

The political practices of Trumpism are far beyond historically "normal" political interaction, debate, or boundaries. By their political oppressions, Trumpism's social persecutors have worked social-political destruction.

They have attacked and adversely affected most American citizens, the voting majority, American democracy, and the freedom-work that God brought about in the nation's historic election. In ways that are immoral, uncivil, lawless, and intimidating, these political persecutors pursued their victims and objective to undermine our democratic society. Here is their Trumpism: **defiant political oppression in its political extreme**.

The spirit of extreme **Trumpism is dragon-like**, and it led to the attempted coup on January 6, 2021, and the nationwide armed political protests in the days following.

On Wednesday January 6, 2021, the nation's political affairs took a wickedly crooked turn. In a planned "Stop The Steal" effort to delay confirmation and overturn the certified Electoral College results of the presidential election by a joint session of Congress, a Trump-incited mob of right-wing and extremist Trumpism supporters' groups and persons forcefully laid siege to the United States Capitol. The resulting Senate's impeachment trial of Trump revealed extensive details and heart-wrenching video of the mob's evil scheme, hateful violence, and attempted assassinations of elected officials that took place during the attempted coup.

While Congress was in session conducting the business of the people, thousands of rioters breached security, stormed the facility, and occupied the chambers and offices of elected officials for hours. Some of the violent and hateful mob carried arms, and law enforcement authorities discovered pipe bombs, explosives, and incendiary devices in the vicinity. For their immediate safety, security personnel whisked away congressional members to secure places on the grounds. At least five persons died in the melee, including a Capitol police officer.

"Incitement of insurrection," "sedition," and "conspiracy" are the terms that legal analysts used to describe this attempted takeover of the national government. The defeated, angry, and unhinged outgoing president was the catalytic instigator behind the coup attempt. Yet, the record should not absolve the president's allies of blame for this historically dangerous and subversive event. These allies included 147 House of Representative leaders and Senators, other Trumpism enforcers, right-wing faith leaders, and certain media outlets. Trump's incendiary rhetoric stoked this anti-democratic evil stratagem for days prior to its occurrence. And he did not take serious action to quell this attack upon an equal branch of America's government. In fact, he called the angry mob "great patriots."

A surge of local, state, district, and federal law enforcement agencies diffused and defeated the insurrection. Congress reconvened in the late evening and continued the constitutional process to certify the results of the Electoral College, the results of which Trump supporters sought to overturn.

Anger, fear, embarrassment, uproar, outcry, sadness, anguish, lament, shock, chills, fright, shame, blame, intercession, and resolve are just a few of the reactions and responses that swept through the hearts of the nation's citizens.

With great justification, many elected and government officials, and other public and private influencers of national affairs began to call for Trump's resignation, second impeachment, or quick removal from office via the Constitution's 25th Amendment.[5]

By the grace of God, democracy in the United States of America dodged a bullet on January 6, 2021. However, if political things do not change, quelling a future coup attempt may not be as successful. Leaders in our nation must do what is necessary to prevent extreme political manifestations of Trumpism and must seek to exorcise this evil spirit from the national ethos.

---

[5] See Jacqueline Thomsen, "'Inciting a Riot': Legal Community Erupts in Calls for Trump's Removal as Mob Storms Capitol. The takeover of the building forced the evacuation of lawmakers, staffers and members of the press," *National Law Journal,* Jan. 6, 2021. https://www.law.com/nationallawjournal/2021/01/06/inciting-a-riot-legal-community-erupts-in-calls-for-trumps-removal-as-mob-storms-capitol/

"[7] Our soul has escaped as a bird from the snare of the fowlers; The snare is broken, and we have escaped. [8] Our help is in the name of the Lord, Who made heaven and earth."[6]

◊ **Trumpism after Trump —
An Extending Crisis and a Cancer**

Trump is out.

He is a defeated former incumbent, ousted from the seat of presidential powers, twice impeached, and tried by the Senate on February 8, 2021. Though acquitted, many—but not enough—justifiably encouraged his conviction.

Biden is in.

He is the inaugurated president, the nation's new, hope-filled leader, and inheritor of a fragile political-social predicament.

The lingering aftermath and political-social erosion left behind by the nation's ex- highest office holder were not erased by the inauguration of the new president. The rancid stench and corrosive effects of Trumpism remain, even as was quite evident in Trump's second impeachment trial. Many Republican Senators were yet fearful to vote to convict the former president even though the violent insurrection he incited threatened their very lives. His acquittal has emboldened him to revengefully exert his terrorizing political-social influence.

The nation's political crisis is yet not over, and most likely will remain to afflict the nation for a long time to come. Though the notorious former president is out of office, he, and the spirit of his Trumpism with its political defiance yet

---

[6] Psalm 124:7–8, NKJV.

remains a formidable force in American politics. **The evil spirit of Trumpism continues** to animate the ex-president and many of his steadfast followers throughout the nation. The practices of Trumpism are cancerous and have metastasized in America's political ethos. **Proponents of democracy must urgently attempt to excise this religion-based, political-social disorder from the nation.**

Millions of Trump supporters remain quite influential. Trumpism supporters numbered over 88.7 million Twitter followers in the nation, not counting those Republican political representatives in Congress. In the final days of his presidency, Twitter justifiably suspended Trump's account. So did other social media platforms that took similar safeguards to curb his ability to incite his followers and core base. Yet, there are other media platforms which are promotive of Trump and sympathetic to the Trumpism ideology. He has expressed an intention to establish his own communications platform to continue reaching and manipulating his loyal base. He is also contemplating forming a new political party to further his vain political ambitions.

The same vindictive and vengeful spirit of their defeated leader continues to drive the perverted thinking and actions of Trump's most loyal, cultish followers. Like him, they refuse to quit their oppressive ways. Prophetic Americans must seriously contend against the spirit and perpetrators of Trumpism for the overall health and well-being of the nation.

"Righteousness exalts a nation, But sin *is* a reproach to *any* people."[7]

"Cry aloud, spare not; Lift up your voice like a trumpet; Tell My people their transgression . . ."[8]

---

[7] Proverbs 14:34, NKJV.

[8] Isaiah 58:1a, NKJV.

Consequences

◊ **Political**

All crises have consequences. Crises precipitated by oppressive political leadership have terrible consequences. The defiant political oppression of Trump and his cultish followers have wide-ranging ramifications. Because of their defiant political oppression, ex-president Trump and his enablers caused or exacerbated deep trouble for millions. Concurrently they failed to adequately address crucial problems facing the nation. The defeated ex-president and his adherents—which includes his unshakable white Evangelical voting base—have acted in uncivil and immoral ways that are dangerous for a nation facing volatile situations and times.

The politically terrorizing effects of Trumpism have victimized leading Republicans, or "Retrumplicans" as some refer to them.[9] Trump holds these elected political leaders as hostages, as his complicit victims. Many of those in high offices who align themselves with the ideology of the defeated president could oppose him, his Trumpism, and his defiant political oppression. Yet many refuse to act responsibly, even after the election of a new president, even after the political violence of January 6.

For over four years and counting Retrumplicans allowed Trump and his tyranny to run wild. They have acquiesced to his belligerent ways since the beginnings of the 2016

---

[9] A term traceable to 2015, referring to a Trump supporter who has abandoned traditional Republican values. Trump has inordinate control over the Republican Party. For example, the party's platform for the 2020 election mirrored Trump himself.

presidential campaign.[10] Prior to the attempted coup, most Republican leaders were hypocritically silent, and they demonstrated their true cowardice and complicity in perpetuating the political crisis. Many continue to fear facing the political ramifications of crossing the ex-president and his millions of enablers who possess enormous political and financial resources and demonstrate a propensity for violence. **They're scared.**

They fear suffering the anger of the ex-president (especially prior to the permanent suspension of most of his social media accounts) who they believe would have targeted them in one of his condemnatory messages that instigate Trump supporters to take revenge. Some fear losing political financial donations which these politicians often use to line their pockets and cushion their lifestyle. Others fear having their political aspirations for a higher office cut short when Trump decides to support and finance an alternative candidate to replace a disloyal Retrumplican. Then there are those who are frightened by the prospect of losing their raw political power. Some are just plain scared for their personal safety and the security of their family. Trump's "We'll-take-care-of-them-for-you" fanatic, right-wing extremists often threaten the lives and relatives of those who break with him.[11]

---

[10] Trump opened his campaign on a very offensive and filthy note: he called Mexicans rapists and drug dealers; caught on tape, he bragged about sexually assaulting women and grabbing them by their genitalia; etc.

[11] Let's not forget the foiled plot (October 2020) to kidnap and neutralize Gretchen Whitmer, the governor of Michigan. Also recall Trump's response (September 2020) to a debate question calling on him to condemn white supremacists and militia groups. He said, of the Proud Boys, a right-wing extremist group:

"[25] Fearing people is a dangerous trap, but trusting the Lord means safety. [26] Many seek the ruler's favor, but justice comes from the Lord."[12]

Understandably, some Retrumplicans—acting as spineless pawns for political oppression—**fear death by the devil**, by Satan. They fear facing the evil Destroyer who terrorizes them with his spiritual powers. The devil entraps these ungodly, political-social cowards and enslaves them in spiritual bondage. Yet, Jesus could emancipate them from all their fears if they would only repent from their Trumpism and trust Him as their LORD.[13]

◊ **Social**

To understand additional grave consequences of neglecting to address a nation beset with crises, we need only to contemplate the tens of thousands of people who have gotten sick and died from COVID-19. The first month of 2021 saw deaths from the coronavirus climb to over 3,500 per day, January 5–8. On the eve of the presidential inauguration the death toll from the coronavirus surpassed 400,000, the horrendous legacy of the disgraced ex-president, Trump.

Consider the financial disaster that has created massive food lines the likes of which Americans have not seen since the Great Depression. When it comes to the labor market, 14.7 million Americans were unemployed in January 2021, and 140,000 persons lost a job in December 2020. Numerous businesses are struggling, failing, and closing for good.

"Stand back and stand by." This was a call for them to be ready to act, forcefully/violently (implied).

[12] Proverbs 29:25–26, NLT.

[13] Jesus can deliver those who are subject to the bondage of the devil because they fear dying and death. See Hebrews 2:14–15.

Think about the educational consequences experienced by our children who must do virtual schooling. Many have fallen behind one or two years in their learning. Consider the uptick in cases of emotional and physical abuse to children and mates when the spreading pandemic required the society to stay-in-place.

Or take note of the feelings of isolation and hopelessness, emotional burdens that daily impact tens of thousands of lives. Understand the climbing rate of suicides in this season of crises; empathize with the loved ones of those who gave up trying to cope with their pain, and simply brought an abrupt end to their life.

◊ **Spiritual**

On the spiritual and Church front, the Name of Jesus has suffered due to the apostatizing support of white Evangelicals for Trump and his Trumpism. As a result, because of this unholy association, the reputation and witness of true Christian faith has suffered deep spiritual consequences. Many genuine followers of Christ, including young and progressively thinking believers, have abandoned their connections to evangelicalism[14] and to other Christian groups and churches—all because of the white Evangelicals who operate as the core base of Trumpism.[15]

---

[14] They prefer identifying terms such as "post-Evangelicals" or "adjacent Evangelicals." See: Nicholas Kristof, "Pastor, Can White Evangelicalism Be Saved? A Conversation about Christmas and Faith's Role in Building a 'Beloved Community,'" *The New York Times,* Dec. 19, 2020. https://www.nytimes.com/2020/12/19/opinion/sunday/christian-evangelical-christmas.html?action=-click&module=Well&pgtype=Homepage&section=OpEd%20Col-umnists#commentsContainer

[15] For an insightful analysis of white Evangelicals and Trump/Trumpism by white Evangelicals who placed distance between themselves and the political-social movement, see the following: Frank Schaeffer, "How White Evangelicals Sold Their Soul

Blatant hypocrisy of white Evangelicals has pressed Black believers of an authentic evangelical variety to publicly clarify their theological, cultural, and social positions on issues that impact African Americans. During the 2016 presidential campaign I addressed this issue in an article about the social-political, if not theological, chasm between white Evangelicals and the overwhelming majority of explicit and implicit Black evangelical voters in the nation. **"Certified Black Evangelicals: 'We Are 'Evangelical' and Political, But Not Whitenized'"** [16] became a predictively prophetic piece.

to Donald Trump to Bring About Armageddon," interviewed by the *Tom Hartmann Program*, May 21, 2018. "Frank Schaeffer, former Evangelical explains how white evangelicals in the United States put faith before country, before human rights, in making a 'Devil's Bargain' to support Donald Trump despite his less than Christian actions, for a handful of policy and power goals . . ." YouTube. https://www.youtube.com/watch?v=CQoxoZn3EpI&feature=youtu.be Reverend Rob Schenck, "Reverend reveals what evangelicals say privately about Trump," Interviewed by Michelle Martin, *CNN*, Jun. 16, 2020. "Reverend Rob Schenck, a former evangelical activist, discusses President Trump's photo-op after police forcibly moved protesters and what evangelicals are now saying about Trump." Young adults are "leaving evangelical churches in droves." https://www.youtube.com/watch?v=lOBh-Hs_1n_I&feature=youtu.be

[16] See Rev. Dr. Walter Arthur McCray, "Certified Black Evangelicals: 'We Are 'Evangelical' and Political, But Not Whitenized.'" https://www.the-nbea.org/home-3/certified-black-evangelicals/ April 5, 2016. The late Juneteenth national advocate and spokesperson, the Reverend Dr. Ronald V. Myers, MD, must receive credit for continually pressing this author and the National Black Evangelical Association to urgently address the identity issue of white Evangelicals/Black evangelicals. The theological-biblical and racial-cultural-social rationale for the article is in *Pro-Black, Pro-Christ, and Pro-Cross: African-Descended Evangelical Identity*, Rev. Dr. Walter Arthur McCray, Chicago: Black Light Fellowship, 2012. https://blacklightfellowship.com/product/pro-black-pro-christ-pro-cross-african-descended-evangelical-identity-paperback/

I first wrote the message when the term "Trumpism" and its ideology were nascent, prior to commentators weaving it into the national political fabric.

The article called for the media to add the descriptive adjective "white" when their reports made reference to the "Evangelical" voting base of Trump. Its aim was to make a clear identity-distinction between the social-political aspirations and values of "white Evangelicals" versus those known to be "certified" Black evangelicals. Not all "evangelicals" were/are Trump and Trumpism supporters. In the intervening years since publishing the article, the truth of making such a crucial identity-distinction became self-evident in the 2016 and 2020 national elections and is a foregone conclusion in 2021—whether or not the media adjusts the way it reports on the issue. The white Evangelical/Black evangelical religious-political divide is a glaring racial-social reality.

Sometimes authentic evangelical Blacks have had to justify or readjust their associations with the wider white Evangelical world.[17] Understandably so. Trumpism has

---

[17] Note the Southern Baptist seminary presidents' view of critical race theory being incompatible with the theology of the denomination. See: Yonat Shimron, "Southern Baptist Seminary Presidents Nix Critical Race Theory," *Religion News Service,* Dec. 1, 2020. https://religionnews.com/2020/12/01/southern-baptist-seminary-presidents-nix-critical-race-theory. Some Blacks have pulled out of the group. See: Yonat Shimron, "Houston Pastor Cuts Ties to Southern Baptists over Critical Race Theory Critique," *Religion News Service*, Dec. 16, 2020. https://religionnews.com/2020/12/16/houston-pastor-cuts-ties-to-southern-baptists-over-critical-race-theory-critique/ See: Leonardo Blair, "Pastor Dwight McKissic says he's leaving SBTC, possibly SBC over critical race theory dispute," *Christian Post Reporter*, Jan. 20, 2021. https://www.christianpost.com/church-ministries/pastor-dwight-mckissic-says-hes-leaving-sbtc.html

hijacked and corrupted the "evangelical" name and white Evangelicalism. By and large, many of its prominent proponents perpetuate Trumpism.

Trumpism adversely effects the ministry of bringing salvation to the lost, to those without Christ—an issue that genuine followers of Jesus must never minimize. The Scripture directly connects the social climate created by the governance of political leaders with the salvation of every person.

> "[1] I urge you, first of all, to pray for all people. Ask God to help them; intercede on their behalf, and give thanks for them. [2] Pray this way for kings and all who are in authority **so that we can live peaceful and quiet lives** marked by godliness and dignity. [3] This is good and pleases God our Savior, [4] **who wants everyone to be saved and to understand the truth.** [5] For, There is one God and one Mediator who can reconcile God and humanity—the man Christ Jesus."[18]

It is without serious debate that the presidential era of Trumpism seriously disrupted the **"quiet"** and **"peace"** of our society. Particularly onerous is Trump's attack and undermining of "truth." In this light, sincere believers must justifiably raise a crucial question: To what extent has the spiritual repercussions of Trumpism become a stumbling block that has hindered the eternal life of those who otherwise would have placed their trust in the LORD Jesus, our eternal Savior? The ungodly alignment of white Evangelicals with Trumpism has impeded the integrity of a Christ-centered witness to Him Who is "the Way, the TRUTH, and the Life" of God incarnate. One day they must give an account for obstructing

---

[18] 1 Timothy 2:1–5, NLT (emphasis added).

the "truth of the Gospel" manifested in Jesus, the Messiah, the Anointed One of God.[19]

The instances cited above are but a few of the political, social, and spiritual consequences that impact American lives and society because of the failed, uncivil, and morally bankrupt leadership of Trump & Co. Trump and his manifestation of Trumpism have become a destructive wrecking ball on American life. Moreover, the post-election unethical and defiant actions of Trump and Trumpism enforcers invite spiritual consequences that are dangerous and destructive for him and his cohorts.

Theology of a Divine Retribution

At this critical national moment, the following question stares our nation in the face: What divine consequences should America expect when defiant political oppressors refuse to let a nation go free? A theological discussion and principle address this question.

◊ God-Directed Punishment

Political actions usually produce consequences, social and otherwise. So also, oppressive political actions produce abnormal conditions, social and otherwise. On the other hand, oppressive political actions may invite God to **miraculously intervene** in the human and societal sphere with remedial acts of a destructive nature.

---

[19] See John 14:6; Galatians 2:5, 14; Matthew 16:16. Some Evangelical Republicans have called out their leaders to acknowledge the truth. E.g., see: Jason Lemon, "GOP Congressman Calls on Christian Leaders to 'Admit Their Mistakes' in Pushing Trump's Conspiracies," *Newsweek,* Jan. 12, 2021. https://www.newsweek.com/gop-congressman-calls-christian-leaders-admit-their-mistakes-pushing-trumps-conspiracies-1560907

In response to sinful political and social activity, God may choose to compound normal/natural adversity with a form of spiritual/supernatural affliction. In such a case, God specifically visits judgments/punishments upon the objects of His wrath for their persistently oppressive ways. Hence, we aptly call this intervention **"a divine judgment"** or a punishment from God. A divine judgment is a special punishment. Such a judgment has **a definitive spiritual dimension, and a direct act of God drives its effects and remedial purpose**.

Every now and then, the Divine allows a rather godless and continuously oppressive leader to rise for a season. Sometimes the will of the Sovereign permits an adverse and adversarial ruler to ascend to power, but only for a while. The Almighty permits the immoral ruler to govern just long enough and rise just high enough for God's miraculous intervention to decisively cut him down. When it happens, most everyone realizes that it was an act of God that brought down the oppressive ruler and liberated the oppressed people. The LORD Himself gets the glory.

An historical precedent that happened just outside the land of ancient Egypt elucidates the divine consequences cited above. I call upon **the Red Sea historical-theological motif** to give witness to this truth. It is the basis of this political discussion and gives credence to its central message. **The Red Sea event directly points to serious and destructive spiritual consequences that persistent politically oppressive elements will come to experience.**

The ruling Pharaoh at the time of Israel's exodus from Egypt met this tragic fate. Ol' Pharaoh's army got drowned in the Red Sea. In the days of the prophet Elijah, both wicked King Ahab and Queen Jezebel of Israel suffered an experience where God terminated their lives. In the days of the prophet Daniel, God also brought down the arrogant Babylonian King Nebuchadnezzar with a sudden and humiliating judgment.[20]

◊ Self-Inflicted Consequences

Persistently oppressive political creatures who precipitate political-social crises effect **spiritual consequences upon their own lives**. Eventually, in this life, they suffer spiritual repercussions for their oppressive ways. Sometimes the Divine orchestrates these spiritual consequences. On occasion, God chooses to act against the adverse and corrupt political practitioners in a nation. Consequently, He directs an extremely wasting and destructive experience to come upon their lives.

Accordingly, based on this same principle, and perhaps sooner than later, a divine judgment may well become the tragic experience of America's oppressive ex-political leader and his operatives. Given the current state of political affairs in the nation, the application of this truth is obvious to many. Perhaps the developments triggering this divine and remedial correction have already begun to unfold, even much sooner than we understood at the time when initially writing this message.

The divine judgment under discussion here focuses on Trump and his immediate Trumpism enforcers. Its scope does not necessarily include all Republican supporters or adherents. The truism is relevant and applicable: "Those who are not a part of the solution are a part of the problem."

---

[20] "I have planned this in order to display my glory through Pharaoh and his whole army. After this the Egyptians will know that I am the LORD!" (Exodus 14:4b, NLT). See Exodus 14:17–18; 1 Kings 16:28—22:40; Daniel 4:1–37.

By persisting in their obstinate ways, Trump and his Trumpism enforcers are inviting a divine spiritual punishment upon their lives. By their behaviors, these political oppressors are inescapably brewing for themselves some type of destructive judgment that will have severe social consequences. They are setting themselves up for a divinely orchestrated and power-breaking intervention. A divine judgment of this nature brings suffering and death. God would design such an intervention to further release the nation from the oppressive political grip and terrorizing actions of Trumpism enforcers.

◊ Democracy-Necessitated Remedy

The tenuous political situation precipitated by the defiant political oppression of extreme Trumpism presumably necessitates a divine intervention as a remedy to preserve the nation's democracy.

The crisis-level political situation in America has been extremely complicated and delicate. Democracy is in danger. Those who endeavor to bring the political crisis to a satisfactory resolution face a high risk. The process of dealing with Trump, even post his term in office, and with the allies of Trumpism, has been fraught with inherent dangers; it has been tantamount to defusing a time bomb. The law enforcement lockdown of the District of Columbia and the nation's Capitol leading up to Biden's inauguration testifies as much.[21] Continuing threats of politically motivated violence there, and across the nation, are very serious.

National matters have threatened to explode in the face of truth speakers, peacemakers, race lovers, justice seekers,

---

[21] See: David Leonhardt, "A Capital Under Siege," *The New York Times*, Jan. 20, 2021. https://www.nytimes.com/2021/01/20/briefing/inauguration-2021-trump-pardons-jack-ma.html

and democracy preservers. Many accept the possibility that America's diversity project could fail. Our democracy could further erode and dissolve. Civil war could envelop the land. Anarchy could spread. It is possible for totalitarianism or authoritarianism via Fascism or neo-Nazism to take hold. The attempted, but failed political coup confirms the possibility that the politics and social affairs of the nation could turn south, and become horrifying. This was an extreme crises situation, and its ramifications remain precarious.

In light of this political minefield, **a divine intervention may very well become the salvation of continuous American life in its best and truest form**.

Here we envision an America of diverse and united people—a multiracial, multicultural, responsible, and accountable society that respects and protects all persons; a nation of opportunity whose truth-filled, justice-filled, and freedom-filled soul prioritizes uplifting the poor, dispirited ones in our midst; an authentic republic that affords a free voice and fair choice for every citizen; and a community that grants the sheltering cover of love and promise for all who covenant to live together in peace.

It is this ideal of America that is worthy of preservation for succeeding generations. And many believe that the good LORD has a compassionate and just interest in delivering such an America from the enslaving clutches of her internal enemies who oppose true democracy.

The high-risk factor of Trumpism that threatens American democracy means that activist believers must keep God at the social-political table. In all our endeavors—whether to promote truth, justice, and freedom; to preserve our nation's democratic way of life; or to maintain our sanity in all our endeavors we must acknowledge the LORD each step of the way.

> "[5] Trust in the Lord with all your heart, And lean not on your own understanding; [6] In all your ways acknowledge Him, And He shall direct your paths."[22]

> "[5] I wait for the Lord, my soul waits, And in His word I do hope. [6] My soul waits for the Lord More than those who watch for the morning— Yes, more than those who watch for the morning."[23]

While as socially-activist believers in Christ we do our part to address the nation's political-social crises, **we must faithfully trust God to miraculously intervene**. We need to seek the LORD and rely upon Him to perform a unique work in our society. We must trust God to bring to pass the kind of deliverance that the Divine alone can perform. Such a divine judgment/deliverance would result in a major change in the quality of life for those who are politically oppressed and socially distressed in our nation.

> "But Moses told the people, 'Don't be afraid. Just stand still and watch the Lord rescue you today.'"[24]

> "Be still, and know that I am God! I will be honored by every nation. I will be honored throughout the world."[25]

---

[22] Proverbs 3:5–6, NKJV.
[23] Psalm 130:5–6, NKJV.
[24] Exodus 14:13a, NLT.
[25] Psalm 46:10, NLT.

God Himself shall rightfully receive the credit and praise for His deliverance. Ironically, the people of God may receive the blame for His judgment!—even from the embittered mouths of those ubiquitous Trumpists and truth-twisting conspiracists!

Given the uncertain state of our currently treacherous political-social affairs, **the favor of a divine retribution may ultimately become the only viable experience that can save our tottering nation from imploding and tearing itself apart at the seams**. America desperately needs an intervention from God to redeem our nation from chaos, to remediate its political-social disintegration, and to preserve her soul from the evil and corrupting forces of defiant Trumpism.

2

Historical-Theological Precedent

A Compelling Sermon

As a minister of the Gospel and a Church pastor, for most of 2020 I consistently prepared a weekly message to proclaim to a small flock of God's people, and to others who tuned in to our virtual worship service. The spirit and drama of national crises and the politically troubling past months provided prophetic preachers with an unfolding—if not overriding—social and political context for their anticipated Sunday messages.

We ministers know too well that our folks long to hear "a word from the LORD," a word that speaks clearly to their personal, cultural, and national situations—one that especially speaks hope to them in times that are quite fragile and uncertain. Our people ask their ministers a question: "Watchman, what of the night?" Or,

> "Night watchman! How long till daybreak? How long will this night last?"[26]

Students of the Scripture often discover irrepressible truths by searching the annals of theologically understood events. Ministers often ask themselves the question: What is a relevant theological and historical precedent that can sufficiently inform the crises-laden situation that tries our souls?

A motif from the history of the Old Covenant people of God energized the sermon I preached immediately following the national election. The historical account of God's deliverance of the Israelites when they crossed the Red Sea, following their exodus from Egyptian bondage, compelled the theme for my Sunday message on November 8, 2020. My text was Deuteronomy 11:1–4, and the message title was "Victory Shall Be Mine."

The Red Sea Motif, the Children of Israel

Reading the words that narrate the Red Sea story provides an apropos theological perspective on the political situation and its aftermath that have gripped our nation.

A single verse of the text theologically spoke and prophesied to my spirit.

---

[26] Isaiah 21:11, The Message.

"[Remember what the LORD] did unto the army of Egypt, unto their horses, and to their chariots; how he made the water of the Red sea to overflow them **as they pursued after you**, and how the LORD hath destroyed them . . ."[27]

"They pursued after you" was the potent phrase that gripped my heart and focused my thoughts. Ol' Pharaoh and his army had **pursued the liberated** Children of Israel, but only to the Egyptians' own destruction. Miraculously, the LORD intervened to protect His recently freed captives. He delivered them from their former captors who had defiantly pursued the nation, even chasing after them into the Red Sea.

The army of Egypt's ruling Pharaoh at the time of the Exodus was the unfortunate casualty of a divinely destructive takedown. God's sovereign power prevailed over the oppressive powers of Ol' Pharaoh.

"For the Scripture says to the Pharaoh, *For this very purpose I have raised you up, that I may show My power in you, and that My name may be declared in all the earth.*" [28]

"But indeed for this purpose I have raised you up, that I may show My power in you, and that My name may be declared in all the earth."[29]

By pursuing the liberated Israelite nation, Ol' Pharaoh and his army were continuing their opposition against the freedom-work of God. Ultimately God brought their oppressive pursuit to a terminally destructive end.

---

[27] Deuteronomy 11:4, KJV, emphasis added.

[28] Romans 9:17, NKJV, emphasis added. Exodus 9:16, NKJV; see also Exodus 14:17; Proverbs 16:4.

[29] Exodus 9:16, NKJV; see also Exodus 14:17; cf. Proverbs 16:4.

The Red Sea Model, the Christian Community

Theological harmony ties together the faith-community experiences of the Children of Israel and the followers of Christ. Early Christian writers of the Scripture use Old Covenant historical precedents as "examples" and "warning-examples."[30] The ancient Israelites' historical Red Sea experience is one precedent within this purview.

Two relevant New Covenant passages mention the Red Sea experience. The initial citation appears in First Corinthians, where the passage mentions the "cloud"[31] and the Red Sea crossing as a baptism into Moses. We can read the passage in two versions:

> "[10:1] Moreover, brethren, I do not want you to be unaware that all our fathers were under the cloud, all passed through the sea, [2] all were baptized into Moses in the cloud and in the sea,"[32]

> "[1] Friends, I want to remind you that all of our ancestors walked under the cloud and went through the sea. [2] This was like being baptized and becoming followers of Moses."[33]

The LORD baptized the Israelites "into Moses." The phrase **"into Moses"** signifies the **purpose** of the Cloud/Red

---

[30] Literally, as a **"type"** and a **"type" of "warning";** see 1 Corinthians 10:6 and 11; Romans 15:4; 2 Timothy 3:16–17.

[31] The "cloud" was God's **presence and protective covering** over the liberated nation as they traveled on their journey of freedom through the Red Sea, in the wilderness, and ultimately into the land of Promise. See, for instance, Exodus 13:21, 22; 14:19–22, 24; Numbers 14:14.

[32] 1 Corinthians 10:1–2, NKJV.

[33] 1 Corinthians 10:1–2, CEV.

Sea baptism. Every baptism has four essential parts. We see these four aspects in the Cloud/Red Sea baptism: 1) the Baptizer was the LORD; 2) the candidates for baptism were the Israelites; 3) the element was the "the cloud and the sea"; and 4) the purpose of the baptism was "into (or unto) Moses," as the leader of the liberated Israelites.

> "[29] But the Israelites went through the sea on dry ground, with a wall of water on their right and on their left. [30] That day the Lord saved Israel from the hands of the Egyptians, and Israel saw the Egyptians lying dead on the shore. [31] And when the Israelites saw the mighty hand of the Lord displayed against the Egyptians, **the people feared the Lord and put their trust in him and in Moses his servant.**"[34]

In this miraculous Cloud/Red Sea baptism, God established/confirmed Moses as His legitimate leader of the newly liberated Israelite nation. No longer were these former slaves subject to, or subjected themselves to, the oppressive rulership of Ol' Pharaoh, but to Moses their divinely appointed liberator. Through the Cloud/Red Sea experience, the LORD completely broke the Israelites' yoke of bondage to their oppressors, and He firmly established Moses as the uncontested leader of the freed nation.

Divinely instituted changes in leadership often accompany a "Red Sea" judgment/deliverance. God replaces ungodly, oppressive leaders, with godlike liberating leaders. For the people whom He frees from injustice, God provides leaders who operate in the spirit of His own heart. In Jeremiah's and Ezekiel's day, the LORD said He would replace the

---

[34] Exodus 14:29–31, NIV, emphasis added; see Acts 7:35–36.

Israelite nation's irresponsible leadership with "shepherds according to My heart . . .".[35] The concept of "shepherd" in these passages included all classes of religious and political leaders. It refers to the collective leadership of the people: priests, prophets, kings, and princes. In historical context, "shepherds" include all the religious and ruling nobility over the nation.[36]

Millions in our nation are quite grateful for the new kind of diverse leadership choices of the Biden administration. There is a great relief for the anticipated changes that the new leadership promises to bring. No one can guarantee the extent of positive outcomes; however, the presidential change has lifted a political burden. Righteous leaders in authority make a big difference in the nation's progress. Their influence and impact are invaluable.

> "[28:28] When the wicked come to power, people hide, but when they are destroyed, the righteous flourish. [29:2] When the righteous flourish, the people rejoice, but when the wicked rule, people groan."[37]

The anonymous author of Hebrews wrote the second New Covenant passage about the Red Sea to an early Hebrew-Christian community. It presents the LORD's Red Sea destructive intervention upon the Egyptian Ol' Pharaoh and his army as a forecasting model for followers of Christ. Based on their faith-obedience, the same type of divine "Red Sea" deliverance was available for the persecuted early Christian community. The following words express this example/exhortation:

---

[35] Jeremiah 3:15, NKJV.
[36] See Ezekiel 34:1–24; Jeremiah 2:8; 10:21; 25:34–38.
[37] Proverbs 28:28; 29:2, HCSB.

"By an act of faith, Israel walked through the Red Sea on dry ground. The Egyptians tried it and drowned."[38]

The writer of the text encouraged the Hebrew believers in Christ who were living in the first century A.D. (those addressed in the book of Hebrews) to place their faith in the LORD when facing the "Red Sea" experiences in their lives. In the like manner of the LORD delivering the ancient Israelites, the writer encouraged these Hebrew believers to trust in God to intercede on their behalf against their persecutors.

In the historical context of the Hebrew Christians, their implied political oppressors were the Ol' Pharaoh of the Roman Empire and his pursuing army. Indeed, hostile Roman authorities persecuted these earliest Christians.[39] Nero was the fifth emperor of Rome, he ruled A.D. 54–68. He was known for his persecution of Christians whom he arrested, tortured, crucified, and burned under his political oppression. The apostle Paul and other believers lost their lives during the time of Nero's reign.[40]

Roman leaders persecuted early believers even as these political authorities had persecuted our Lord, Jesus the Messiah. Herod Antipas, a Roman political ruler of mixed Jewish ancestry, had also wrongfully treated the Forerunner of our faith. The oppressive political Judean representative

---

[38] Hebrews 11:29, The Message.

[39] See Hebrews 10:32–34; 13:3; Philippians 1:12–13, 28–30; 1 Peter 4:12ff.

[40] R. F. Youngblood, F. F. Bruce, & R. K. Harrison, *Nelson's New Illustrated Bible Dictionary*, Thomas Nelson Publishers (Eds.), Nashville: Thomas Nelson, Inc., 1995; M. T. Griffin, "Nero (Emperor)," In *The Anchor Yale Bible Dictionary*, Vol. 4, D. N. Freedman, (Ed.), New York: Doubleday, 1992, p. 1080.

of Caesar's Rome, Pontus Pilate, ultimately tried and crucified the Lord as a common criminal.[41]

In matters concerning the social-political persecution of God's people, in any historical period God may choose to achieve His redeeming purpose by acting to effect a "Red Sea" type of deliverance. In a miraculous way, He can decisively bring judgment upon the pursuers/persecutors of those who are seeking freedom from social-political oppression.

The Self-Destructive Pursuit of Ol' Pharaoh's Army

Carefully consider Deuteronomy 11:1–4, the text which recounts the Israelite Red Sea deliverance from Egyptian oppression.

Moses is speaking to the Children of Israel. He focuses their attention on what God had done for His people in the time of their bondage in Egypt land. Thus, in these words Moses reminds the Israelites of

> ". . . the **chastisement** of the LORD your God, his **greatness**, his **mighty hand**, and his **stretched out arm**, [3] And his **miracles**, and his **acts**, which he did in the midst of Egypt unto Pharaoh the king of Egypt, and unto all his land;".[42]

In the context of His redemptive works, Moses sees the LORD as a Warrior-Deliverer God. This is His nature.

"The LORD is a warrior; the LORD is his name."[43]

---

41 On Herod and Pilate, see Luke 23:1–15ff.; Acts 5:25–27; Luke 3:1; John 19:8–16; 1 Timothy 6:13.

42 Deuteronomy 11:2b–3, KJV, emphasis added.

43 Exodus 15:3, KJV.

Recall the story of the exodus of the Israelite nation from Egypt. When the Israelites were living in Egypt, God performed mighty works to redeem His people from their oppression. Moses spoke for the LORD and commanded Pharaoh to set free the Children of Israel. During a series of confrontations and divine plagues, Pharaoh would first grant the nation their freedom. Afterward he would change his mind and reverse his decision. The story indicates that, in several different instances, Pharaoh vacillated with his decision to free the people.[44]

The final and crippling straw was the 10th plague that God sent upon Egypt. This judgment eventuated in the death of the firstborn in every home that the Israelites had not covered with the blood of a sacrificial lamb. This was the night of the Passover.[45]

On that terrible night of the Passover judgment/pre-servation, Pharaoh once again decided to fully release the Israelites from their bondage. However, after he freed his captives and they left the land of Egypt, Pharaoh once again changed his mind. He continued having second thoughts about letting the captives go free. Consequently, Pharaoh commanded his army to pursue the liberated nation. This is what the sacred text indicates when it reads, **"they pursued after you"**.[46]

Pause for a moment to think about the situation. The LORD had continually pressured Pharaoh to set God's

---

[44] See Exodus 8:8 and 15; 8:25 and 30; 9:28 and 35; 10:8 and 11, 20; 20:24 and 27.

[45] See Exodus 11:1–12:30.

[46] Deuteronomy 11:4, KJV, emphasis added. See Exodus 14:23; 15:9.

people free. However, Pharaoh and his army did not completely surrender to God's will. Instead, they doubled down in their defiant resistance to God's deliverance. Consequently, the Word tells us that Pharaoh's army continued to pursue the liberated nation. In essence, they **"persecuted"** the freed Israelites. Though the power of God had already defeated this oppressive Pharaoh, in common parlance, he yet refused to "concede" defeat.

Instead, in an act of stubborn rebellion, Pharaoh and his army **sought to overturn the freedom-work of God** by attempting to bring the liberated nation back into the bondages of social oppression. Their actions were foolish, causing a fatal judgment that they brought upon themselves at the Red Sea. Ol' Pharaoh and his army made their own deliberate choice to unwisely pursue (and obstinately persecute) their victims. They even chased their fleeing former captives into the divinely dried-up seabed. Eventually, God used Moses to cause the waters of the Red Sea to return and overflow Pharaoh's army, and they drowned. [47]

Pharaoh's army could have escaped this judgment. They could have avoided their meeting with death in the Red Sea. They should have taken a different course, and I believe they would have, if they only could have perceived the unfortunate fate that awaited them. I believe that God would have spared the lives of Pharaoh's army if they had decided to **cease pursuing the liberated nation**.

Tragically, however, Pharaoh's army sealed their own destructive destiny by continuing their asinine pursuit. Moreover, the egotism that led to the deaths of these soldiers

---

[47] Exodus 14:5ff., 26–27; 15:4, 9, 10, 19; Psalm 106:8–12; Hebrews 11:29.

had much wider ramifications. Imagine the loss felt by their parents, widows, children, extended family members, and friends. What grief, pain, and great suffering they experienced with the drowning deaths of their loved ones.

A Divine Pattern Emerges

The historical record of God's miraculous judgment upon Ol' Pharaoh's army at the Red Sea, and His deliverance of the liberated former captives, stands as is. Yet, the actions of Ol' Pharaoh and his army, who defiantly pursued the Israelites, is telling. Here we learn a lesson that is eye-opening: it is unwise and extremely dangerous to continually persecute oppressed people who have been set free by God.

Sometimes an oppressive leader and his enforcers just won't quit. **They persecute, they pursue, and they die.** The divine pattern is clear: 1) decisive liberation from oppression; 2) defiant pursuit by the oppressors; and 3) divine intervention of destructive judgment. The Warrior-Deliverer God ultimately prevails against any forces that attempt to impede or thwart His redemptive work of freedom and justice.

In this motif, we discern a clear theological and spiritual truth. Implicitly this principle warns all oppressive national leaders—whether those of the U.S. or other nations—of the dire consequences of facing an impending divine judgment for continually pursuing those whom God has set free from oppression and injustice. The idea is relevant for appraising the social-political situation that has unfolded in America. This principle highlights the direction and pathway toward which the political affairs of our nation have trended, even during the crucial days and weeks that have followed the presidential election. A type of spiritual destruction awaits anyone who persistently and defiantly attempts to reverse or overthrow the liberating works of God.

"One who becomes stiff-necked, after many reprimands will be shattered instantly—beyond recovery."[48]

---

[48] Proverbs 29:1, HCSB.

3

America's Freedom, Ol' Pharaoh and His Army, and the Red Sea

Ex-president #45, and his political enforcers, have evinced that they are a modern-day type of Ol' Pharaoh and his pursuing army. They are defiantly oppressive. They are persistently provocative and pushing the political affairs of the nation to an extreme crisis. Seemingly they are pursuing the political ends of Trumpism despite the cost to the welfare and future of a democratic America. Ultimately, if they persist with their political persecution, they will encounter a judgment-intervention of God at the "Red Sea."

I.

Decisive Liberation from Trumpism Oppression

◊ Oppressive/Toxic Trumpism

The oppressive nature of the ex-president is well attested. Reflecting on his personhood is eye-opening. His shameful character and damaging actions are despicable, and disgraceful. He is known to lie and deceive continually; he is anti-truth. He is immoral. He is racist, misogynistic, and mean-spirited. He stokes the violence of race haters. He is the kind of materialistic leader who pads the pockets of those who are already filthy rich. His god is money and the values of materialism.

Trump is a vile man who is full of himself and has a debilitating, deep-seated narcissism. He is privately, publicly, and abrasively sinister. He is full of hubris, the kind of arrogant pride that opposes true humility—and defies God. The ex-president is an obvious and obnoxious sinner. He is bound by his iniquity of lawlessness, yet he refuses to genuinely repent, or to unambiguously relent. He is defiant.

The nation's ex-president is politically, morally, and spiritually toxic. And his toxicity has infected millions of his Trumpism adherents. He easily instigates them to commit acts of anger and violence against their "enemies." His tendency to incite a race war in America is not beyond the reasonable thinking of many who analyze America's racial situation.

Together, Trump and his allies are a contemporary model of the oppressively defiant Ol' Pharaoh of Egypt, and his pursuing army. Consequently, by their persecutory words, actions, and political oppressions, they are opposing the freedom-work of God. And they are inviting the LORD's judgment upon themselves.

◊ Ten Oppressions/Evils of Trumpism (Chart)

In the presidential election, many intentionally voted against the manifest character of Trumpism's oppression. The chart below lists 10 aspects of Trumpism and the values that oppose this ideology.[49]

---

[49] Rev. Dr. Walter Arthur McCray, "'Trumpism' Opposed by Evangelical Black Values," Chicago: Black Light Fellowship, © 2018, 2021, Walter Arthur McCray.

10 Oppressions / Evils of Trumpism

"Trumpism" is a Spirit —an Evil Spirit.

The spirit of this ideology manifests itself in ungodly words, attitudes, actions, and policies . . . in a "wisdom" that is not from above, but in an anti-spiritual mentality that is "earthly, sensual, and devilish."

James 3:15

Black Evangelical Values are Spiritual Weapons.

This armor fights against the devil's stratagem and schemes manifested in "Trumpism": "For we wrestle not against flesh and blood, but against spiritual wickedness in high places."

Ephesians 6:10–13ff.
2 Corinthians 6:7; 10:4–5

1

Lies and Deception

"Trumpism" says, "If I can, I'll tell the 'truth.'" Or "I'll lie and get away with it."

Truth

As truth-tellers we follow Jesus, Who is the truth; and He taught that the truth sets us free.

John 14:6; 8:32

Hubris, Arrogance	2	Humility Before the Lord, Jesus Christ
"Trumpism" is pride that is opposite humility; it says, "I am the only one that matters." "I am the only one who can fix it." This hubris exalts self-reliance, and self over others; it is an affront to God—Who does not share His glory with another.		We submit to the LORD, Who is God Alone, All-knowing, and Almighty. God opposes the proud. 1 Corinthians 1:29–31 Philippians 2:9–11 James 4:6
Biblical, Historical Ignorance	3	Historically Factual Biblical Education
"Trumpism," with its white Evangelical theological proponents, erroneously assume that biblical and early Church history are white and Eurocentric, and this illiterate and perverted notion negatively impacts their dealings with people of color.		Learning about the Black/African biblical presence and Africa's shaping of the earliest Christian faith is essential education for decentering, resisting, and correcting Evangelical whiteness and supporters of "Trumpism."

Racism, White Supremacy, White Nationalism	**4**	**Black Christian Cultural Internationalism**

"Trumpism" is a "nationalist" ideology, meaning a white supremacist nationalism. A "form of godliness" undergirds this ideology, and its intransigent adherents manifest a cultish spirit. This white identity ideology evokes fear and provokes oppressive and violent behavior toward non-white people.

Advocating pro-Black self-affirmation and determination in Christ protects, preserves, and empowers people of African descent, amidst white racism, supremacist practices, and white privilege. Loving God, Black people, and others is Christ-like and commanded by the Lord.

Isaiah 58:7
Matthew 22:39
Philippians 4:8

Divisive, Incendiary Rhetoric and Practices	**5**	**Peacemakers**

"Trumpism" foments discordant divisions that target racial groups (Blacks/African), ethnic entities (Hispanic), and otherwise; it incites hateful actions, and calls neo-Nazis "very fine people."

God blesses peacemaking, collaboration, and reconciliation; He hates divisive practices.

Proverbs 6:16–19
Matthew 5:9

Misogyny "Trumpism" brags about objectifying and assaulting females.	**6**	**Female Co-Equality and Community with Males** All males must consecrate, respect, receive as equals, and protect all females. Genesis 1:26–28 Ephesians 5:28–31
Partiality to the Rich "Trumpism" grants favors and disproportionate tax cuts for millionaires and billionaires; disfavoring, not prioritizing the poor.	**7**	**Good News for Poor People** Jesus came to "Gospelize the poor," and to set the captives free; His true followers effect the same for the least in society. Luke 4:18–19
Immigrant Insensitivity "Trumpism" godlessly impedes immigrants and destroys families, inhumanely and heartlessly separating children from parents.	**8**	**Reception of Foreigners** Welcoming "strangers" (or immigrants, aliens) is welcoming Jesus, and shows hospitality. Matthew 25:35–40 Romans 12:13 Hebrews 13:1

Anti-Media Bias	**9**	Prophetic Voice
"Trumpism" demonizes certain reporters, i.e., so-called "fake news" media persons, and suggests that its followers subject them to violence and mistreatment; it especially disrespects and demeans Black media persons and consciousness-raising social activists.		Speaking God's truth to power, and for the voiceless in society, is our prophetic calling; we expose lies and disseminate truth; Black evangelical forums and media support and facilitate this ministry. Proverbs 31:8–9; 24:8–12 Isaiah 58:1 2 Timothy 2:24–26
Refusal to Repent	**10**	Repentance and Correction
"Trumpism" makes no apology or remedy for offenses, manifesting spiritual and moral obduracy.		Reversing ungodly attitudes and behavior, and rectifying wrongs, are spiritually righteous practices. Acts 17:30; 26:20 2 Peter 3:9

◊ True Freedom Comes from God

Believers in Jesus the Christ—I am one of His Gospel-izers—must never forget that true freedom and freedom from oppression are the work of God. Jesus proclaimed the following truths:

> "And ye shall know the truth, and **the truth shall make you free.**"

> "If the Son therefore shall make you free, **ye shall be free indeed.**"

> "[18] 'The Spirit of the Lord is upon Me, Because He has anointed Me To **gospelize the poor.** He has sent Me to heal the brokenhearted, To proclaim **liberty to the captives** And recovery of sight to the blind, **To set at liberty those who are oppressed**; [19] To proclaim the acceptable year of the Lord.' "[50]

In the words of a Black spiritual, the **I AM** God gave the liberation command to Moses His servant: *"Go down, Moses, way down in Egypt land. Tell Ol' Pharaoh, let my people go."*[51]

◊ Freedom by Overwhelming Vote

In the 2020 U.S. presidential campaign, God was setting the nation free from the tyrannical oppression of an ungodly and unfit political leader. On the night of the presidential election (and the days of tallying the votes that followed), the picture began to emerge of God giving freedom to our nation from the ironclad grip of President #45, and his cultish followers and minions in power.

---

[50] John 8:32, 36; Luke 4:18–19, NKJV, literal; emphases added.
[51] H. T. Burleigh, "Go Down, Moses (Let My People Go!)" in *Negro Spirituals* (New York: G. Ricordi, 1917). https://library.duke.edu/digitalcollections/hasm_no708/ See Exodus 3:10; 4:22; 5:1; 6:10; 7:2; 8:1; 8:28; 9:1.

Most of the truth-, justice-, and freedom-seeking American people spoke loud and clear by their historic vote. They decisively rejected the incumbent and denied him a second four-year presidential term. Yet, a nuance appeared in their voting pattern. Even while Republicans increased their numbers in Congress but saw their control in the Senate decreased by losing two key Senate runoffs in Georgia, President Biden overwhelmingly won the popular and Electoral College votes against the incumbent.[52] Many of us believe that the hand of God was in the mix in the outcome of that historic vote, unfolding His will to displace Trump.

In the election, a multitude of honest and determined voters raised high their collective voice to oppose President Trump's blatant executive order that prohibited diversity and anti-racist training, dialogue, language, and ideas. Dealing with issues of systemic racism as defined by critical race theory[53] was high on their priority. Based on the election's outcome, most of the country's voters rejected Trump's racism, misogyny, white nationalism,[54] and the

---

[52] Biden won the Electoral College votes, 306 to 232; and the popular vote, 81.2 million (51.4%) to 74.2 million (46.9%).

[53] Critical race theory is an ideology that helps to identify and define systemic racism. It is a major component of anti-racism and diversity training. President Trump's executive order in September 2020 labeled it as a "destructive ideology." *Executive Order 13950*, "Combating Race and Sex Stereotyping," *Law and Justice*, Sept. 22, 2020. https://www.federalregister.gov/documents/2020/09/28/2020-21534/combating-race-and-sex-stereotyping

[54] Let's never forget Trump's infamous words on the protest and anti-protest confrontation in Charlottesville, VA (Aug. 15, 2017) when he declared, "you also had people that were very fine people, on both sides." On one side were those who had courage to stand against those on the other side who were spreading hate: racists, neo-Nazis, David Duke of the KKK, alt-right groups, white supremacists, a terrorist who committed murder with his car, etc.

authoritarianism as manifested in his bent toward Fascism and neo-Nazism.[55]

The nation should be grateful, and never overlook, that so many Black people—and Black Church women in particular—who live in several swing-state cities and suburbs led the voters' movement in the election by their mail-in ballots or their in-person presence at the polls. They did so in cities like Philadelphia, Detroit, and Atlanta. President Biden and his capable governing mate—Lthe Black (and Christian) woman of color and south Asian descent—Vice President/Senator Kamala Harris—won the free election fair and square.

References made above to Black Church women and Christian, Vice President Harris, highlight the "evangelical" stance of many who voted against Trump and his white Evangelical supporters. By virtue of their participation in Black churches and based on their faithful practices of essential Christian beliefs, African Americans, implicitly

---

[55] Trump has demonstrated an appalling deference to the Russian autocratic leader Putin, and to autocrats of other regimes such as North Korean dictator Kim Jong Un; Turkish President Recep Tayyip Erdogan; and others. See: Chris Cillizza and Brenna Williams, "15 times Donald Trump praised authoritarian rulers." *CNN*, Tue. July 2, 2019. https://www.cnn.com/2019/07/02/politics/donald-trump-dictators-kim-jong-un-vladimir-putin/index.html Domenico Montanaro, "6 Strongmen Trump Has Praised — And The Conflicts It Presents," *NPR*, May 2, 2017. https://www.npr.org/2017/05/02/526520042/6-strongmen-trumps-praised-and-the-conflicts-it-presents Zeynep Tufekci, "America's Next Authoritarian Will Be Much More Competent: Trump was ineffective and easily beaten. A future strongman won't be." *The Atlantic*, Nov. 6, 2020. https://www.theatlantic.com/ideas/archive/2020/11/trump-proved-authoritarians-can-get-elected-america/617023/

considered, are the most "evangelical" group in the nation.[56] Black believers as a collective line up more closely with historical evangelical beliefs and practices than do others in the nation.[57]

Explicitly identified white Evangelicals may have voted for Trump, but surely not the implicitly identified Black "evangelical" followers of Jesus. En masse, the swing-state votes of Black believers must receive the credit for throwing the incumbent, unfit Trump out of his undeserved presidential office. And we believe that the hand of God orchestrated this liberation movement by Black Christian voters. The same holds true for the victories of the two Senate runoff races in Georgia on January 5, 2021. Black believers and especially African-American church women were instrumental in the wins of both Democratic candidates.

$$\text{\cfbraces}$$

---

[56] The Institute for the Study of American Evangelicals at Wheaton College states that certain estimates of the number of U.S. Evangelicals "tend to separate out nearly all of the nation's African American Protestant population (roughly 8–9% of the U.S. population), which is overwhelmingly evangelical in theology and orientation **(for example, 61% of blacks–the highest of any racial group, by far–described themselves as "born-again" in the 2001 Gallup poll)**" (emphasis added). http://www.wheaton.edu/ISAE/Defining-Evangelicalism/How-Many-Are-There [accessed 3-14-2016]. Sarah Eekhoff Zystra, "Pew: Evangelicals Stay Strong as Christianity Crumbles in America," *Christianity Today*, May 11, 2015. http://www.christianitytoday.com/gleanings/2015/may/pew-evangelicals-stay-strong-us-religious-landscape-study.html [accessed 3-19-16]

[57] They are "born again," believe all the Bible is God's Word, consider themselves "*Gospelizers*"—"'**Good News messengers**' of the resurrected Lord, Jesus Christ"—and adhere to other essential tenets that help to define evangelical faith.

II.

Defiant Pursuit by Dragon-like Persecutors

Malicious internal forces drove the ancient king of Egypt to oppress and pursue his liberated former captives, the Israelites. The same pursuing spirit possesses and animates the oppressively and politically defiant ex-president and his cultish adherents to Trumpism, along with their worst manifestations. They are oppressive pursuers of those who voted for justice and freedom from the tyrannical rule of the ex-president. They seek to overthrow the freedom-work of God by recapturing an America that is breaking free from the political oppression of Trumpism.

◊ **The Satanic Dragon and Dragon-like Trump/Trumpism**

Defiant actions of pursuing/persecuting are satanic in nature. Such a temperament and practices reveal the spirit of the "evil one," even the "dragon" of the book of Revelation. Depicted in Revelation 12, the dragon is "**terribly angry**" or "**enraged**." It is the defeated dragon who continually pursues to destroy God's redemptive work and who persecutes His people.[58]

> "Then the dragon was **enraged** at the woman and went off to **wage war** against the rest of her offspring—those who keep God's commands and hold fast their testimony about Jesus."[59]

---

[58] See Revelation 12:3, 4, 7–8, 13, 16, 17. Cf. 1 Peter 5:8, the devil prowls around as a devouring lion.

[59] Revelation 12:17, NIV, emphases added. See also the CEV.

Basic dragon-like characteristics define someone who is **fiercely vigilant** or **intractable**; **formidable** and **dangerous**; **violent** and **combative**. Any political oppressors who fail to relent from a mindset and practices of pursuit/persecution manifest the spirit of the dragon.

Looking back, we see that both the pre- and post-election demeanor, actions, and stratagem of Trump and his forces substantiate their dragon-like nature. The extremely negative traits and actions of America's Ol' Pharaoh became quite apparent when he first ascended to the presidency. However, post-election matters and developments further revealed and exacerbated the Ol' Pharaoh-like moral and ethical corruptness of the nation's then-sitting chief political leader, and his crowd.

Trump's post-election calculated maneuverings are a predictive sign. They forecast the demise of this terribly unfit yet defiantly oppressive ex-leader and his enforcers—save only for their repentance and the mercy of God.

Jesus gave a warning to those living in His generation. He predicted the destructive consequences that would come upon those who pursue/persecute others.

> "[49] Therefore the wisdom of God also said, 'I will send them prophets and apostles, and *some* of them they will kill and persecute,' [50] that the blood of all the prophets which was shed from the foundation of the world may be required of this generation, [51] from the blood of Abel to the blood of Zechariah who perished between the altar and the temple. Yes, I say to you, it shall be required of this generation."[60]

---

[60] Luke 11:49–51, NKJV.

In a relevant biblical incident, the teacher Gamaliel gave a sharp warning to some persistent pursuers/persecutors of the early followers of Jesus:

"[38] 'So my advice is, leave these men alone. Let them go. If they are planning and doing these things merely on their own, it will soon be overthrown. [39] But if it is from God, you will not be able to overthrow them. You may even find yourselves fighting against God!'"[61]

One might also consider the fateful experience of Haman the Agagite, or Haman the "flame," a reference to his **anger, fury**. To his own eventual demise, furious Haman pursued/persecuted Mordecai, and his people the Jews. Haman's own officials ended up handing him on the very gallows that he had constructed for Mordecai, his intended victim.[62]

Ex-president Trump manifests the nature of Haman, for it is common knowledge that he has a serious problem with his angry and erratic temperament. In this regard, Trump is a dragon-like fool. Why? Because

". . . **anger abides in the heart of fools**."[63]

Close friends of angry Trump are likewise foolhardy for associating with him: **they set a trap for their own soul**:

"[24] Make no friendship with an angry man, And with a furious man do not go, [25] Lest you learn his ways And set a snare for your soul."[64]

---

[61] Acts 5:38–39, NLT.

[62] See the book of *Esther* and Esther 3:1–6; 5:9; 6:4; 7:1–9. D. L. Christensen, "Agag (Person)," In *The Anchor Yale Bible Dictionary* Vol. 1, D. N. Freedman (Ed.), New York: Doubleday, 1992, p. 88. See also Proverbs 29:1.

[63] Ecclesiastes 7:9b, HCSB.

[64] Proverbs 22:24–25, NKJV.

◊ The Dragon's Destructive Tail

Let's consider the backstory of extreme Trumpism. Here we review the nature and effects of Trump's dragon-like political persecution, and the broad sweep of its destructive tail.

> "His tail swept away one-third of the stars in the sky, and he threw them to the earth."[65]

We can observe four areas of interrelated defiant actions of the nation's dragon-like ex-leader, and his complicit social oppressors: a) he deifies himself and demagogues God's freedom-work; b) he defies and defames the voting majority; c) he desecrates and denies the populace; and d) he devalues and damages our precious democracy.

a) Deifying Himself and Demagoguing God's Freedom-Work

The word "cultish" is an appropriate term that aptly describes adherents to Trump and Trumpism. Trump's rallies, with their thousands of fanatic supporters, have a characteristic religious fervor. The manifestly unextractable allegiance of white Evangelicals to Trump—to immoral, ungodly Trump—testifies to their misplaced spiritual allegiance. Often, they see him in the role of the biblical "Cyrus," or even as their "savior."[66]

---

[65] Revelation 12:4a, NLT.

[66] See: Adam Gabbatt, "'Unparalleled Privilege': Why White Evangelicals See Trump as Their Savior," *The Guardian,* Jan. 11, 2020; https://www.theguardian.com/us-news/2020/jan/11/donald-trump-evangelical-christians-cyrus-king "'Q' and Their Questionable Messiah," *Chicago Crusader,* Sept. 1, 2020; https://

Many Christians view biblical characters as inspirational leadership models for their lives or their causes. That's okay. However, **when we juxtapose such models alongside Trump and his Trumpism, with its demand for absolute loyalty or fealty, herein lies the problem.** When these believers further conceptualize and relate to Trump as their "Messiah," then at this intersection **the theological apostasy and spiritual scandal has run its full course and has corrupted Christ-centered faith.**

By wrapping their affections around such conceptions, many white Evangelicals open themselves to the practice of idolatry.[67] In their Christian ethos, they have supplanted Jesus the Christ and His way with a theological-spiritual attachment to Trumpism, and the relationship is harmful and destructive. **They cling closer to Trump and his teachings than they follow the Lord, our only Savior.**[68] Their corrupted form of the Christian faith, with its white patriarchal and political dominance, is **not authentic Jesus**, and is dying.[69]

chicagocrusader.com/q-and-their-questionable-messiah/ Gregory Alan Thornbury, "QAnon's 'Messianic Secret,'" *Religion and Politics*, October 22, 2020. https://religionandpolitics. org/2020/10/22/qanons-messianic-secret/

[67] See: David French, "The Dangerous Idolatry of Christian Trumpism: We Can Pray Peace Will Prevail, But We'd Be Fools to Presume it Will," *The Dispatch*, Dec. 13, 2020. https://frenchpress. thedispatch.com/p/the-dangerous-idolatry-of-christian?utm_ campaign=post&utm_medium=email&utm_source=copy

[68] At the stop-the-steal rally that precipitated the failed coup, protestors carried signs such as "Trump is my savior, Jesus is my president." See: Jason Lemon, "Over 16,000 Christians Want Franklin Graham Fired for 'Helping Incite' Capitol Riot," *Newsweek*, Jan. 19, 2021. https://www.newsweek.com/over-16000-christians-want-franklin-graham-fired-helping-incite-capitol-riot-1562632

[69] See: Richard T. Hughes, Op-Ed: "The ferocious last gasps of the religion of Christian America," *Los Angeles Times*, Jan. 19, 2021.

The apostle Paul testified of this sort of religious apostacy when he wrote these words:

> "For [although] they hold a form of piety (true religion), they deny and reject and are strangers to the power of it [their conduct belies the genuineness of their profession]. Avoid [all] such people [turn away from them]."[70]

Trump has deified himself in the eyes of millions; he has taken the place of God in their lives. He has become to them a demagogue, a political leader who has deceptively won their support by appealing to their desires and prejudices rather than by using rational argument. Trump's errant personal and social-political behavior substantiates the irrationality of his demagoguery.

His past actions told us that President Trump has the kind of self-justifying and self-centered temperament that would allow him to make any power and vindictive moves. His actions were exemplifying a god-like persona, with attendant privileges and powers.

Ol' Pharaoh and his army, with their post-election antics, operated under the guise of seeking fairness. In the face of Biden's resounding victory, they kept spreading lies, and "The Big Lie"[71] that promoted outlandish conspiracy theories about the election. Millions of the ex-president's deluded followers steadfastly believed his every tweet. Whether he downplayed the coronavirus, dispensed with

---

https://www.latimes.com/opinion/story/2021-01-19/christian-right-john-calvin-white-supremacy-patriarchy

[70] 2 Timothy 3:5, ANT.

[71] See Hitler's use of "the big lie" or the stratagem to "fabricate colossal untruths." https://en.wikipedia.org/wiki/Big_lie#Hitler's_use_of_the_expression

wearing protective face masks, slammed the so-called "fake news," or incessantly prefabricated a "stolen election," they hung on to any words uttered from his very deceitful lips.

Trump is a "deceiver," and he and his Trumpism syco-phants are also self-deceived because they reject the truth. Scripture identifies this spiritually reprobate state:

> "[10] . . . They perish because **they did not accept the love of the truth** in order to be saved. [11] For this reason **God sends them a strong delusion** so that they will believe what is false, [12] so that all will be condemned —**those who did not believe the truth but enjoyed unrighteous-ness.**"[72]

Despite the nation embarking on its journey toward a renewed freedom, this Ol' Pharaoh and his army just wouldn't quit. Even prior to election day, this Ol' Pharaoh had begun to pursue his political ends in ways that were extremely evil-minded, oppressive, vengeful, and defiant. No surprise, for this is the real-real identity of the persecutor, even prior to his "day one" in office, in 2016.

The defeated president and his operatives set their sights on **recapturing those who had received freedom from their oppressive policies, practices, programs, and tactics**. Their underlying motives aimed to undermine freedom, and to position themselves to retain or regain power. In the days that followed his resounding defeat, the worst of the man appeared and began to wreak havoc in the nation. His atti-tudes and actions became a devilish terror.

---

[72] 2 Thessalonians 2:10b–12, HCSB, emphases added.

b) Defying and Defaming
the Voting Majority

It is a terrible thing to victimize a people by defying their right to choose freedom. It is a worse thing to castigate victims by accusing them of possessing corrupt character and actions that render them deserving of their own victimization. Trump has committed both evils. **He has defied and opposed the choice of freedom by the majority of the nation's voters, and he has defamed the righteous character of these freedom- and justice-seeking voters by casting and castigating them as election stealers.**

For an extended period following the election, the national waters remained restless and uncertain—on all fronts. Newly inaugurated President Biden had received a resounding victory at the polls on November 3, 2020. Yet in typical fashion, the defeated president, Trump, immediately began to obstinately double down.

The rejected ex- refused to concede defeat. So also did most of his sycophants, prior to November 23, or until the Electoral College declared their results. Nevertheless, conceding defeat is not tantamount to abandoning Trumpism. Some Republicans who at that time reluctantly affirmed Biden as the president-elect, or who now accept him as the nation's new president, continue to support Trump and his Trumpism ideology. Many of these lawmakers became objectors to the Electoral College's certification of the states' voting results. A good number opposed his second impeachment and fought against a conviction.

Time and time again, Trump blatantly accused Democrats of "massive voter fraud," "voting irregularities," and "rigging" and "stealing" the election—patently false accusations which, astoundingly, 70 percent of his loyal-to-a-fault Republicans indignantly choose to believe. Trump appealed to the basest desires and prejudices of his followers. Many of the things he said and did were irrational, yet his loyalists have steadfastly stood by the defeated ex-president. He unjustifiably declares that the election was "rigged."

Despite the true numbers that declared their candidate the political loser, an overwhelming number of the 73+ million Trump voters chose to keep following the deceptive and defiant lead of their defeated incumbent. Trump, by virtue of his high profile, radicalized-conservative mindset, and his demagoguery, has provided validation for their suspicions that a stolen election "**might** be true."[73] Yet, the 2020 election was declared to have been the "most secure in U.S. history" by the Cybersecurity and Infrastructure Security Agency (CISA) of the Homeland Security Agency. There "is no evidence that any voting system was deleted or lost votes, changed votes, or was in anyway compromised," stated Chris Krebs, the director of CISA.

Trump promptly fired him for contradicting the false conspiracy theories of his defeated boss. Yet, Krebs left with courage and integrity. Soon after, a Trump campaign lawyer made a public (a so-called hyperbolic) death threat

---

[73] Ross Douthat, "Why Do So Many Americans Think the Election Was Stolen? Looking for Reasons Behind a Seemingly Unreasonable Belief," *The New York Times,* Dec. 5, 2020; https://www.nytimes.com/2020/12/05/opinion/sunday/trump-election-fraud.html?action=click&module=Opinion&pgtype=Homepage Leib Litman, et al., *Cloud Research Survey*, Nov. 6, 2020. https://www.cloudresearch.com/resources/blog/americans-divided-over-election-fraud-2020/

to the official's life. Persecutory words matter. The director and his family needed special protection. So also did other election officials who worked to uphold the fairness and security of the people's votes. Trump's supporters made threats on their lives also. Trump supporters and right-wing media outlets even accused the principals of two companies that provided the voting machine systems to tabulate voting results in certain states. Trump enforcers attacked them for conspiring to digitally fix the election, a patently false accusation.[74] On January 25, one company filed a $1.3 billion defamation lawsuit against Trumpism enforcer Rudy Giuliani.[75] These business professionals have also received threats.

Trump has defamed the character of those who swore officially to uphold election laws, and he has refused to speak out against those who threaten violence against these officials.

Trump's campaign lodged at least 62 court challenges related to the election results, only to have 61 of these totally baseless cases dismissed, settled, withdrawn, or denied one

---

[74] Kiran Stacey, "Voting Machine Group Demands Retractions from Rightwing Media," *Financial Times,* December 24, 2020. https://www.ft.com/content/fb20bab6-9135-4ed6-a64e-ade85b0eee18

[75] See, Associated Press, "Dominion Voting System sues Giuliani over election claims: The lawsuit seeks more than $1.3 billion in damages for the voting machine company, a target for conservatives who made up wild claims about the company, blaming it for Trump's loss," *POLITICO,* Jan. 25, 2021. https://www.politico.com/news/2021/01/25/dominion-voting-system-giuliani-election-462122 See, Olivia Rubin, "Voting machine company files $1.3B suit against pro-Trump attorney Sidney Powell, who pushed false election claims," *ABC News*, Jan. 8, 2021. https://abcnews.go.com/US/voting-machine-company-files-13b-suit-pro-trump/story?id=75132589

after another.[76] His lawsuits have failed. To their dismay, recounts and audits of vote totals did not uncover any widespread fraud or corruption in the election. The state of Georgia (re)certified its voting totals in favor of Biden three times. The U.S. Supreme Court twice refused to hear the irrational arguments of Trump's legal representatives.

In vain, the modern-day Ol' Pharaoh and his army sought to overturn the election results. Their intention was to subvert and undermine the democratic process, and the justified protection of legal voting. They made threats and filed numerous legally baseless lawsuits. On the federal, state, and local levels, they mounted failed legal challenges to the obvious electoral outcome in favor of President Biden. In their vindictive political crosshairs, led by Trump, they brazenly targeted millions of Black voters who live in concentrated locales and sought to overturn Blacks' liberating votes. But nothing stuck.

The ex-president continued to oppressively defy the will of the people. The U.S. Supreme Court refused to hear one case of Trump's campaign that sought to undermine the clear will of the people in the election. The Justices

---

[76] William Cummings, Joey Garrison and Jim Sergent, "By the numbers: President Donald Trump's failed efforts to overturn the election": Trump and allies filed scores of lawsuits, tried to convince state legislatures to take action, organized protests and held hearings. None of it worked. *USA TODAY,* Jan. 6, 2021. https://www.usatoday.com/in-depth/news/politics/elections/2021/01/06/trumps-failed-efforts-overturn-election-numbers/4130307001/ Pete Williams and Nicole Via y Rada, "Trump's Election Fight Includes over 50 Lawsuits. It's not Going Well," *NBC News,* Nov. 23, 2020. https://www.nbcnews.com/politics/2020-election/trump-s-election-fight-includes-over-30-lawsuits-it-s-n1248289

simply wrote, "Denied." Another case submitted by Trump and his allies to the Supreme Court enlisted the support of numerous states' attorneys general. The state of Texas led the way by seeking to have the nation's highest court to overturn the voting and election results of swing states. This case also failed.

The defeated incumbent and his enablers continually challenged the political victory of America's majority at every turn. He did not let up. Due to the incendiary rhetoric of Trump toward the members of the Electoral College, several of them had to receive special protection in the process of declaring their vote totals.

A one-hour call of Trump to Georgia's Secretary of State, released by *The Washington Post* on January 3, 2021, reveals Trump's continual attempt to defy the voting majority. The astounding and berating words of the defeated incumbent pressured the Georgia official to "find" enough Trump votes to overturn the state's election results. This desperate tactic opens the ex- to federal or state criminal charges, including election fraud.[77]

Trump's political maneuverings projected his intention to continually perpetrate his defamation and defiance deeply into the ethos of national politics, even into the

---

[77] See Amy Gardner, "'I just want to find 11,780 votes': In extraordinary hour-long call, Trump pressures Georgia secretary of state to recalculate the vote in his favor," *The Washington Post*, Jan. 3, 2021. Trump pressures Georgia's Raffensperger to overturn his defeat in extraordinary call. See David Knowles, "Trump's 'less-than-perfect' call to Georgia officials could also be a crime," *Yahoo News*, Jan. 3, 2021. https://www.yahoo.com/news/trumps-lessthanperfect-call-to-georgia-officials-could-also-be-a-crime-221455096.html

2024 presidential election season. His political persecution is dragon-like, unrelenting.

c) Desecrating and Denying
the Populace

By embarking on his course of political pursuit/persecution, **Trump has desecrated the populace, treating them less than human as created by God**.

We must remind ourselves of a theological truth: the historic record number of millions of righteous voters who decided against political tyranny are bearers of the *Image of God*. These proactivist millions of democracy proponents are the very "offspring of God,"[78] despite their suffering the consequences of having been politically persecuted and held hostage by today's Ol' Pharaoh and his army.

True Christian believers adhere to truths written in the defining sacred documents of our faith tradition. The God-breathed eternal Word admonishes each of us to remember and respect that God's offspring includes ALL persons and peoples—whoever they are. God created and formed ALL persons in the image of the Divine.[79] In the eyes of God, He created all humanity sacred and free; and we should consecrate and treat all persons and peoples with human dignity.

Trump sought to deny the people their inalienable rights of "life, liberty, and the pursuit of happiness" as bestowed by humanity's Creator and which governments should protect. The nation's Declaration of Independence and Constitution affirm these truths. They are America's

---

[78] Acts 17:28–29.
[79] See Genesis 1:27; James 3:9.

"promissory note to which every American was to fall heir," according to the Reverend Dr. Martin Luther King. Spoken over 50 years ago, Dr. King's prophetic words condemn the present practices of ex-president Trump and Trumpism practitioners as those who perpetuate America's default on the moral obligation to deliver on her promissory note.[80]

During the post-election period, the COVID-19 pandemic, with its sicknesses, hospitalizations, and death toll, continued to run wild, even though the government gave emergency approval for vaccine distribution. The economic consequences of this health crisis continue to financially cripple millions of families and business owners. People have suffered for months while longing for additional much-needed financial stimuli from the federal government. On the racial front, cultural undercurrents of yet unsettled systemic Black racial matters have continued to swirl. Politically, extreme proponents of the nation's deep political divide have been ready to unleash intimidating dynamics that threaten reactionary social violence.

Amidst it all, Trump, in his non-caring way, made no good attempt to alleviate the nation's suffering. Moreover, through his incessant challenges to the electoral outcome in favor of Biden, Trump became counterproductive. The actions and inaction of the outgoing president have

---

[80] "In a sense we have come to our nation's capital to cash a check. When the architects of our republic wrote the magnificent words of the Constitution and the Declaration of Independence, they were signing a promissory note to which every American was to fall heir. This note was a promise that all men would be guaranteed the inalienable rights of life, liberty, and the pursuit of happiness. It is obvious today that America has defaulted on this promissory note . . ." Delivered by Dr. King on the steps of the Lincoln Memorial, Washington, D.C., August 28, 1963.

exacerbated the crises, besetting the suffering masses and stoking violent responses against intimidated election officials and others.

Years and days prior to election day, Trumpism supporters sought to legally suppress and deny the votes of Blacks, other people of color, immigrants, students, the elderly, and people with disabilities. Using sinister voter suppression tactics, Retrumplicans made frontal attacks in states such as Ohio, Georgia, Florida, Michigan, New York, Illinois, California, and Pennsylvania. They targeted cities such as Detroit and Boston. Their suppression stratagem against voting empowerment included the following: voter ID restrictions, voter registration restrictions, voter purges, felony disenfranchisement, gerrymandering, armed people at the polls, false robocalls, setting ballot boxes on fire, changing or closing polling places, and the like. Trump's attempt to overturn the Electoral College results was simply an extension of the low-down and disenfranchising ways of Trumpism's voter suppression.[81]

This Ol' Pharaoh and his army turned resentfully angry about the election's outcome, and they have directed

---

[81] See: Voter Suppression, *ACLU*. Feb. 3, 2020. https://www.aclu.org/news/civil-liberties/block-the-vote-voter-suppression-in-2020/ Nicquel Terry Ellis, "Guns, lies and ballots set on fire: This is voter suppression in 2020," *USA TODAY,* Oct. 29, 2020. https://www.usatoday.com/story/news/nation/2020/10/29/2020-election-voter-suppression-looks-like-guns-lies-and-fires/6044702002/ Charles M. Blow, "Supreme Leader of Voter Suppression, Trump is bolstering anti-patriotism in the digital age," *The New York Times*, Jan. 3, 2021. https://www.nytimes.com/2021/01/03/opinion/trump-voter-suppression.html; Justin Worland, "How the Trump Campaign Is Trying to Suppress the Black Vote," *TIME,* Oct. 22, 2020. https://time.com/5902729/black-voter-suppression-2020/

their angst against millions of Americans—Democrats, Republicans, and Independents; African-Americans, other people of color, and whites—who voted against their oppressive rulership. They pursued (i.e., persecuted) the nation's majority—the 81+ million majority who voted to reject autocratic rule and to reclaim freedom from repression and oppression. Trump sought to deny them their God-given freedom and victory.

Trump deeply instilled his supporters with the fear of losing power. When they could, and as much as they could, they tried to hold the nation with its electoral processes as hostages to their insatiable greed for power. These political suppressors and oppressors are perverse and crooked. **They adamantly seek to legally force the American populace into an illicit political submission of the many to the few.** But their devious moves have not worked.

Up until the inauguration of President Biden on January 20, the nation reeled and braced itself. From November 3, 2020 to January 20, 2021, the nation endured several nail-biting weeks of an unhinged lame duck president.[82] He positioned himself to exercise his executive powers in ways that made us cringe. Our questions swirled.

What kinds of actions could we have expected from the time-limited chief executive officer of our nation? How deeply embedded in his psyche was his mindset that refused

---

[82] "All the while, the country lacks a president who has both the power and willingness to reduce the death, illness and mayhem." See, David Leonhardt, "A Cascade of Crises: The U.S. is dealing with a cascade of crises during the wait between a presidential election and inauguration," *The New York Times,* Jan. 8, 2021. https://www.nytimes.com/2021/01/08/briefing/elaine-chao-trump-capitol-neil-sheehan.html

to accept the reality of his defeat? Would he start a distractive international conflict? Would he begin to purge high government officials whom he considered disloyal, and replace them with others who would mindlessly do his bidding? Would he refuse to gracefully depart from his White House residence when it was his time to go? To what extent would he use the powers of his office to force the nation into a constitutional crisis? **Would he instigate his extreme followers to start a race war?**

The mob action and attempted coup of January 6 demonstrates that any of these conceivable actions or moves were a real possibility, or even probability. Dragon-like Trump commended the insurrectionists as they seized, rampaged, and desecrated the offices and meeting spaces of the nation's legislators.

How Trump handled the matters of p**ardons and commutations**, and how he failed to adequately address the COVID-19 pandemic, **further reveal his desecration of America's people**.

High on the priorities of his executive actions were presidential pardons and commutations. Trump intended to use his broad pardoning powers to buy the silence and continued loyalty of his close associates and the political operatives in his inner circle. These executive actions would amount to a massive cover-up of unlawful and criminal activities. His plans to issue pardons/commutations for specific persons were public knowledge, for he telegraphed his intentions. Everyone knew that it was only a matter of time before the watershed moment of demoralizing pardons/commutations would break loose from the presidential office. With the Constitution providing cover, gatekeepers could not do a thing to stop this unbridled miscarriage of legal justice. Since it was legal, we could only protest and watch the outgoing president unfold this travesty—watch with disbelief and disgust.

The manner that the on-the-way-out president chose to use the powers of presidential pardons is one obvious example, among many, that has revealed the true, unethical, and criminal content of his character. Though the pardoning powers of an outgoing president are constitutionally legal, inside knowledge about several pardons/commutations that Trump intended to grant left many of us with a foul, unclean feeling. He placed previously convicted felons, and others charged with federal crimes but had not yet gone to trial, on his likely-to-be-pardoned list. Besides these, he also discussed granting preemptive pardons to his children, his personal attorney, and even to himself.

The outgoing president, true to having telegraphed his intentions, first issued a highly questionable pardon to an otherwise soon-to-be tried associate.[83] This associate had already pleaded guilty to federal charges. He confessed to lying to the FBI about his international relationships and wrongdoing. In the course of time, the courts would have given him a clearly deserved felony conviction. Trump's pardon got his partner off the hook and abetted his escape from serving prison time. It also helped to shield the ex-president from facing his own legal exposure for suspected criminal activity.

Trump designed for his pardons and commutations to freely flow. He sidestepped the usual procedure of having

---

[83] The former National Security Adviser, Michael Flynn.

the Justice Department review the cases of potential pardon candidates. The purpose of such a review is to recommend cases to receive mercy and justice. They ascertain whether a miscarriage of justice had occurred in any case. If so, then the criminal would be a suitable candidate for receiving a pardon. Also, whether a criminal had expressed remorse for the crime that was committed would be a factor for one receiving mercy. Many of those pardoned, or whose sentences the president commuted, expressed no remorse for their criminal activity; they felt justified in taking their law-breaking actions. Trump pardoned them anyway.

Eventually, the soon-to-be-gone president would issue pardons to a good number of his operatives who had been political associates in his inner circle. Several of these recipients are privy to the secret and private dealings of their former boss. Information they know could have led to Trump's impeachment on additional charges aside from "incitement of insurrection," and to his conviction. Their knowledge about inside affairs could most likely lead to Trump's indictment for criminal activity, either on federal or state charges. In effect, the on-the-way-out president chose to use presidential pardons/commutations as "hush money."

The floodgates of presidential pardons burst wide open on December 22 when the outgoing president freely issued 20 get-out-/stay-out-of-jail passes to his sycophants. They were but the first wave of his controversial releases. The second wave came a day later. On December 23, 29 persons received a pardon or clemency. Friends of the president, family, and noncooperative witnesses in the Mueller Russia investigation surrounding Trump's election were part of the group, as had been true of his first wave of pardons. The third wave of pardons came on January 20, 2021. Trump pardoned 74 persons and gave clemency to 70. Included in the mixed-bag of pardons was Trump's strategist, Steve Bannon. He was awaiting trial in Manhattan on federal fraud charges tied to a border wall fundraising effort. The evidence of his crookedness was apparent. Disgusting. Many of Trump's pardons took on the spirit of presidential "obstruction of justice." He has rewarded lawbreakers.

Though legal, many of the pardons he issued were immoral, and very crooked in the eyes of equitable justice. We can only imagine the kinds of thoughts that race through the minds of the thousands of Blacks who are the subjects of mass incarceration. Many of these longtime prisoners whom prosecutors convicted (sometimes unjustly) are serving time for crimes that have a lesser impact on the nation's people than those of Trump's convicted cronies. Regrettably, these brothers and sisters must linger behind bars while the ex-president freely releases his loyal partners-in-crime.

Also, the people of Iraq and the U.S. were outraged when Trump's pardons released four persons convicted of war crimes against innocent Iraqi civilians whom they murdered en masse. Moral outrage and disgust flared up against the president for his immoral subversion of the justice system and his support of this inhumane act of international terror that took place in 2007. His pardons meant that he allowed paramilitary Blackwater contractors to get away with an international massacre.[84]

---

[84] See: "Trump Pardon of Blackwater Iraq Contractors Violates International Law – UN," *Reuters*, Dec. 30, 2020. https://www.reuters.com/article/us-iraq-blackwater-un/trump-pardon-of-blackwater-iraq-contractors-violates-international-law-un-idUSKBN294108

Early in 2020, President #45 knew the truth about COVID-19 and its deadly effects and potential for rapidly pervading the nation. Yet, while in office he gave up on protecting the masses of our people from this pandemic—from this wasting plague that has infected millions and has killed hundreds of thousands. Instead, as revealed in uncovered emails, the administrative policy of the White House opted to pursue "herd immunity" from the coronavirus without a vaccine that would protect recipients from illness and death. They decided to allow the pandemic to simply run its course among the population—a foolish policy that, had they fully implemented it, would have led to the deaths of millions more Americans.

In review, Trump left his presidential successor to inherit a devastating disease against which Trump's administration had not prepared a national plan to counteract. Were the ex-president's actions of dumbing down on the pandemic virus deliberately aimed to afflict Blacks and other people of color whose lives the disease disproportionately affected? The unsettling thought is plausible.

A gnawing uneasiness makes us wonder when we contemplate the real possibility that the ex- "neglector-in-chief" would withdraw enthusiasm by not advocating for the good health-care practices of a Black population that was already more at-risk to catching and dying from COVID-19 than his own white racial group. These disturbing thoughts about the ungodly actions of Trump have a way of stirring up a deep-seated, righteous anger within the souls of all decently civil, ethical, and moral people. His irresponsible failure to act on the coronavirus engenders within us a raw, holy rage.

Crises alarm bells have been screaming across the nation as the coronavirus spread wildly throughout our land. Even while the America that Trump executively oversaw wasted away with disease, death, and financial ruin, he pathetically preoccupied himself with monitoring television news channels for coverage about himself. Or he casually resorted to a golf course with his sickening, loyal-at-any-cost followers. Compared to the number of COVID-19 infections and deaths experienced by other nations, a terrible number of Americans have become needlessly sick or died under the uncaring "watch" of Trump.

d) Devaluing and Damaging Our Precious Democracy

Trump has devalued and damaged the very democracy which elected and installed him in the nation's highest office. **The ex-president and his enforcers have attacked and eroded decent and democratic values, and they have deconstructed revered governmental traditions, policies, and institutions.** They have painfully damaged the lives of some of the nation's exceptional leaders who have sacrificially adhered to the absolute best ideals of American society—truly seeking freedom and justice for all.

A unique political crisis-situation gripped the nation in 2020. An on-the-way-out president encumbered the nation by actively and egotistically seeking to undermine the nation's democracy. It has been hard to wrap our minds around this awkward and alarming situation. This political persecution was **an unfettered and uncharted attack on American democracy**.

As we attempted to get a good handle on these matters, the nation suffered from an absence of social, political, and legal precedents that could have provided sure guidance and beacons of light into a foreseeable stable future. Relative to external and internal dynamics taking place, leaders in high places began to voice their deeper concerns about our national security. Many who tried to get a good grasp of the political and social milieu could not say for certain what the immediate future held in store for the nation.

The nation was traveling through new political and legal territory. Much was uncharted and precipitated rigorous contention. According to some experts, the nation had drawn close to a constitutional crisis. The fast-moving political developments were changing rapidly. We learned to hold our breath, for on any given day, we knew that something unexpected could happen at any time. Things could have quickly turned south and messy—politically, financially, socially, racially, or otherwise.

Rather than quickly and cooperatively passing the governing powers to a new administration, the defeated president worked to obstruct a peaceful transition. He acted to undermine the nation's democracy and fair electoral processes. He gleefully began to reap his socially corrupting crop. In the pre-election period, he had intentionally cast a widespread shadow of political mistrust for the voting process. After the election he began to savor the fruit of these poisonous seeds that he had sown early in the campaign.

For as long as he could get away with it, this calculating president refused to release the General Services Administration to provide the necessary funding and guiding support that is crucial for transferring governing power to the next administration. He, and the GSA administrator, acted as though they could not ascertain the apparent winner of the election two or three days after November 3. They unashamedly committed obvious obstruction and continued the practice during the transition period.

Early on, Trump stridently and uncaringly blocked his people from providing critical information to the then president-elect. For weeks Trump deprived his successor of key substantive briefings on intelligence, national security, and COVID-19 inner-workings. This information was vital for developing a coordinated response to the pandemic and for keeping a watchful eye on America's war zones across the globe. Trump's seat-of-the-pants and mean-spirited reactions were jeopardizing lives at home and abroad.

Nevertheless, the on-the-way-out president continued to hinder the equitable rule of law. Though soundly defeated, he kept instigating his cultish followers to resist the election's outcome. In the meanwhile, he continually sought to delegitimize the nation's incoming president, and to destabilize (sabotage) the new administration. As late as December 28 in the transition period, President-elect Biden accused the Trump administration of hollowing out important government agencies by making them "short on personnel, capacity and morale." The policy processes of these entities were "atrophied" or "sidelined."[85]

---

[85] See, Philip Ewing, "Biden Faults 'Roadblocks' as His Team Manages Transition from Trump," *NPR,* Dec. 28, 2020. https://www.npr.org/sections/biden-transition-updates/2020/12/28/950898048/biden-faults-roadblocks-as-his-team-manages-transition-from-trump

President #45 never intended to invite nor welcome his successors Biden and Harris into the White House. He was adamantly determined to not work enthusiastically for a civil transfer of power. He was determined to not decently aid a peaceful transition of government into the hands of the nation's incoming president and administration. He refused to attend the inauguration of the next president.

Political pressures may have expediently forced the soon-to-be-gone president to correct some of his snake-in-the-grass ways. Yet, the people still could not trust him. Their justifiably wary eyes viewed any seemingly positive changes of attitude the defeated ex- made after November 3, and especially following the attempted coup of January 6. All his apparent movements toward a better direction were suspect. In hindsight, we were right to subject his actions to "wait-and-see" standards. Critical analysts sought to protect the public from Trump's deceptive pattern of calculated bait-and-switch hypocrisy, even when he said that he would work for a peaceful transition. Any compliant actions of Trump were for himself, not to benefit the nation.

Though the proverbial handwriting was already visible on the wall shortly after November 3, the nation patiently waited for the certification of the actual vote totals. The canvassers of the Electoral College were waiting (until December 14) to fulfill their role by casting their votes according to the will of the people. Initially, the process required them to wait for each state to certify the vote totals and pass these along to the state's secretary of state (by December 8). They then sent the certified information along to the state's Electoral College members who met to seal their Certificates of Vote before passing them on to the

Office of Federal Register and the Congress who did their part on January 6, 2021. The defeated incumbent exerted his spirit of defiance and intimidation every step of the way in the political process.

Given the very troublesome situation, many imagined what might be the short- or long-term repercussions for the people of the nation, for the national political landscape, or for our nation's democratic future.

The outgoing executive selfishly pursued his political and financial ends despite the cost to millions of lives. Pre-suspension of his Twitter account, he kept tweeting deceptions and unwarranted firings of key civil and national security government officials. He continued to attack public officials, even those honest Republicans who disagreed with his underhanded practices. He and his operatives blindly ignored the price that Americans would pay then and later for their irresponsible actions. During the transition period, the ex-president raised millions of political dollars from his rabid supporters—monies that he could later syphon and redirect for Trumpism purposes. In plain sight he fleeced his duped supporters. Many simply ignored the abuse, while their selfish leader bankrolled his political brand and uncertain future.

The week of December 14, 2020 found some of the defeated president's forces proffering the idea of invoking martial law in the nation, as a means of retaining the outgoing president's time in office. These taken-to-be-very-serious conversations and debates took place in the media, and in the Oval Office of the White House in the presence of Trump. Some analysts perceived the conversations as a dog whistle for far-right Trumpism operators to incite and commit violent action throughout the nation. At that point, the president could then declare martial law to quell the disturbances, to set aside the election results, and to remain in office. In effect, this would amount to a political coup, and further rupture a divided nation.

In a vain attempt, Trump even sought to use Vice President Pence as a complicit sycophant in overturning the election results when presiding over the Electoral College's certification process. When the vice president refused to buckle beneath the inflammatory and profanity-laced pressure of his boss, **Trump publicly turned against Pence with a vengeance**. In the presidential-incited insurrection, the vice president and his family narrowly escaped capture by the mob who took forceful occupation of the nation's Capitol and the House chamber on January 6. Law officers were fortunately able to whisk away the vice president, legislators, and others to secret and secure hiding places. The angry rioters who repeatedly chanted "Hang Pence" missed their intended target by mere seconds.

As he schemed his exit from office, Trump's negative actions intensified, perhaps revealing a secret stratagem for vengefully inflicting pain on his personal and national opposites. Warnings of his sabotaging the next administration were highly believable, and confirmable. Though a practitioner of self-delusion and fact-denial, this defeated president knew that his time to "reign" was short, for the wheels of a constitutional democracy had numbered his days in the presidential office.

During this critical hour of national change, we found ourselves burdened with a non-appearing, and deafeningly silent, on-the-way-out president who situated himself in the confines of his White House bunker. We could only imagine him plotting some despicable political countermoves designed to preserve himself and his perverted brand. Sure enough, Trump hatched a failed scheme to oust the acting Attorney General and replace him with a sycophant from the Justice Department in order to get the election results overturned. DOJ senior officials thwarted this sinister plan for effecting a political coup by threatening to resign en masse.[86]

Ol' Pharaoh and his army just wouldn't quit. A sulking and tantrum-throwing spirit possessed these losers and abetted their refusal to step aside and allow the nation and our institutions to chart anew our deserved freedom, civility, and rightness. True to conformity to the uncivil actions of their past four years of governing, these obstructionists pursued persecution, sometimes insanely. History will note them as disrupters and subverters of the democratic process and the ultimate good of the country. They are insurrectionist, conspiracist, and seditionist political persecutors. They share the nature of the oppressive "dragon," the satanic destroyer.

03

---

[86] See, Katie Benner and Catie Edmondson, "Pennsylvania Lawmaker Played Key Role in Trump's Plot to Oust Acting Attorney General," *The New York Times,* Jan. 23, 2021. https://www.nytimes.com/2021/01/23/us/politics/scott-perry-trump-justice-department-election.html See, Lauren Booker and Globe Staff, "Schumer says alleged Trump plot to remove acting attorney general is 'unconscionable,' calls for investigation," *The Boston Globe,* Updated Jan. 23, 2021. https://www.bostonglobe.com/2021/01/24/nation/schumer-says-alleged-trump-plot-remove-attorney-general-is-unconscionable-calls-investigation/

III.

Divine Intervention, Destructive Consequences

◊ A "Red Sea" Prophetic Word

The historical Red Sea event of divine judgment and deliverance is a worthy paradigm for our contemporary political situation. The lesson gained from interpreting socio-political happenings from a theological perspective, one that connects with a pertinent historical precedent, speaks clearly and directly to our turbulent political situation.

The trajectory in the Red Sea types/examples prophetically points to the coming acts of God in our day. The same type of Red Sea experiences in the lives of our ancestors of faith is applicable to us—including the many genuine believers who contend with the politically oppressive situation in America. New Covenant believers living in our nation should seek to receive from God the benefits demonstrated in this liberating event. Preservation is the momentous issue at hand in our nation and is pertinent and persistent. We must trust God to prevent any further erosion of our political and social freedoms.

For we too struggle to resist and overcome the oppressions of Ol' Pharaoh and his persistent political enforcers who influence our national affairs. As recently freed former political captives, most in America are attempting to cross our own "Red Sea." Ol' Pharaoh's army of obstinate Trump allies are still in hot pursuit. They would like to punish and regain control of those who have escaped their oppression. The violent riot and attempted coup on January 6, 2021 attests to this truth.

Based on the aforementioned theological-historical precedent, the political crisis in our nation raises uneasy and risky questions for those who are spiritually minded. One question is crucial: What are the divine consequences for the American Ol' Pharaoh and his army when they have resolved to not let God's people go free?

In this light, persecutors who persist in their political, social, and racial oppressions stand to suffer divine judgment for their continuing direct defiance against the gracious but angered face of a Warrior-Deliverer God.

"The Lord is a warrior; Yahweh is his name!" [87]

The High God is the Creator of humanity, and the Sustainer of all life. He is LORD of all.[88] The sacred good will of the LORD desires to break all the yokes of social, political, racial, and spiritual oppression that bind the victims of injustice. Surely, the LORD will act to protect the humanity whom He created.

> "Weeping may endure for a night, But joy comes in the morning."[89]

> "[1] God stands in the divine assembly; he administers judgment in the midst of *the* gods. [2] 'How long will you judge unjustly and show favoritism to the wicked? *Selah* [3] Judge *on behalf of the* helpless and *the* orphan; provide justice *to the* afflicted and *the* poor. [4] Rescue *the* helpless and *the* needy; deliver *them* from the hand of *the* wicked.'"[90]

---

[87] Exodus 15:3, NLT, emphasis added.

[88] See Acts 10:36; 17:7.

[89] Psalm 30:5b, NKJV.

[90] Psalm 82:1–4, LEB.

A theology of the LORD's divine providential oversight assures us that He can and wills to freely care for His own. Through it all, God promises to surely preserve the people whom He has redeemed. And we know that He will. For with God, all things are possible.

◊ Acts of Faith-Obedience

It is the responsibility of the oppressed to genuinely petition and engage with God, the Warrior-Deliverer. In any given historical situation, the LORD anticipates that oppressed people will demonstrate **acts of faith-obedience to secure His miraculous deliverance**.

> "But without faith it is impossible to please Him, for he who comes to God must believe that He is, and that He is a rewarder of those who diligently seek Him."[91]

The Red Sea experience revealed spiritual weakness in the recently liberated Israelite nation, a weakness that almost derailed their deliverance. Their weakness was **fear-rooted rebellion**.

> "[10] As Pharaoh approached, the people of Israel **looked up and panicked** when they saw the Egyptians overtaking them. They cried out to the Lord, [11] and they said to Moses, 'Why did you bring us out here to die in the wilderness? Weren't there enough graves for us in Egypt? What have you done to us? Why did you make us leave Egypt? [12] Didn't we tell you this would happen while we were still in Egypt? We said, 'Leave us alone! Let us be slaves to the Egyptians. It's better to be a slave in Egypt than a corpse in the wilderness!' ' [13] But

---

[91] Hebrews 11:6, NKJV. Cf. Hebrews 11:29.

Moses told the people, '**Don't be afraid.** Just stand still and watch the Lord rescue you today. The Egyptians you see today will never be seen again. [14] The Lord himself will fight for you. Just stay calm.' "[92]

One of the historical psalms confirms this description of the people's reaction at the Red Sea event:

"[6] Like our ancestors, we have sinned. We have done wrong! We have acted wickedly! [7] Our ancestors in Egypt were not impressed by the Lord's miraculous deeds. They soon forgot his many acts of kindness to them. Instead, **they rebelled** against him at the Red Sea. [8] Even so, he saved them— to defend the honor of his name and to demonstrate his mighty power. [9] He commanded the Red Sea to dry up. He led Israel across the sea as if it were a desert. [10] So he rescued them from their enemies and redeemed them from their foes. [11] Then the water returned and covered their enemies; not one of them survived. [12] **Then his people believed his promises.** Then they sang his praise."[93]

An experience of divine deliverance/judgment awaited the recently liberated but pursued former captives. Yet, they had to overcome their fear and retrogressive rebellion in order to receive this miraculous work from God. The lesson learned is that divine deliverance/judgment demands that the pursued/persecuted people exercise their faith and move forward. The LORD honors an oppressed community who place their trust in Him, while they follow the liberating leaders that God has provided for them.

---

[92] Exodus 14:10–14, NLT, emphases added.
[93] Psalm 106:6–12, NLT, emphases added.

The historical precedent is clear: "By faith" the liberated Israelite nation passed through the dried seabed of the Red Sea. Their obedient faith moved them to the action of walking to their deliverance on the other side of the sea.

> "[15] Then the Lord said to Moses, 'Why are you crying out to me? Tell the people to **get moving!** [16] Pick up your staff and raise your hand over the sea. Divide the water so the Israelites can walk through the middle of the sea on dry ground. . . .[21] Then **Moses raised his hand** over the sea, and the Lord opened up a path through the water with a strong east wind. The wind blew all that night, turning the seabed into dry land. [22] So the people of **Israel walked** through the middle of the sea on dry ground, with walls of water on each side! . . . .[26] When all **the Israelites had reached the other side**, the Lord said to Moses, 'Raise your hand over the sea again. Then the waters will rush back and cover the Egyptians and their chariots and charioteers.' . . . .[29] But the people of **Israel had walked** through the middle of the sea on dry ground, as the water stood up like a wall on both sides. [30] That is how the Lord rescued Israel from the hand of the Egyptians that day. And the Israelites saw the bodies of the Egyptians washed up on the seashore."[94]

Faith-obedience is a spiritual response to oppression, and this response invites the **I AM** God into the mix of the struggle for freedom and justice. By placing our trust in a just God Who liberates the captives, we free up His all-powerful hands to act on our behalf. We release God's mercy and His mighty outstretched arm to perform a

---

[94] Exodus 14:15–16, 21–22, 26, 29–30, NLT, emphases added.

wonder-working and liberating redemption for all who suffer social and spiritual oppression.[95]

Whatever else oppressed people see fit to do to resist their oppression and secure their full freedom, it is crucial that they respond to social-political oppressions and aspire to breakthroughs of liberation with acts of faith-obedience in the LORD.

◊ Divine Victory Assured

A verse that sings of victory by means of divine deliverance speaks to keeping up our hope as we wrestle with the implications of America's political-social crises as defined in this message. The words of "Victory Shall Be Mine" (by the late James Cleveland) give spiritual encouragement to those of goodwill.

Victory Shall Be Mine[96]

Verse 1

> *If I hold my peace, let the Lord fight my battles;*
> *I know that the victory shall be mine,*
> *victory shall be mine.*

Verse 2

> *If I walk upright, all my battles He will fight;*
> *I know that the victory shall be mine,*
> *victory shall be mine.*

These words of hope and encouragement capture the thrust of this theological-political discussion and give us

---

[95] Exodus 3:9–10, 14.

[96] Rev. James Cleveland, "Victory Shall Be Mine," *Lyrics on Demand*. https://www.lyricsondemand.com/r/revjamesclevelandlyrics/victoryshallbeminelyrics.html

guidance in our quest for God's intervention, judgment, and deliverance. It is imperative that we *hold our peace,* be still from anxiety and agitation. We must proactively and societally *live upright.* Then we must deeply affirm within our souls that *God will fight our battles* in His own time and unique ways. With hope in our hearts, we must proclaim and prophesy the coming *victory* of God over the defiantly oppressive political operatives in our land.

> "Thus saith the LORD unto you, Be not afraid nor dismayed by reason of this great multitude; for the battle is not yours, but God's."[97]

> "Ye shall not *need* to fight in this *battle*: set yourselves, stand ye *still*, and see the salvation of the LORD with you . . ."[98]

◊ God Watches, We Wait

In a season of national unrest, those who are theologically and spiritually astute are confident that the omniscient God is carefully watching all affairs on the nation's political horizon. In the Red Sea event, the LORD was watching the critical developments of pursuit/persecution by Ol' Pharaoh's army:

> "[19] **Then the angel of God**, who had been leading the people of Israel, **moved to the rear of the camp**. The pillar of cloud also moved from the front and stood behind them. [20] The cloud settled between the Egyptian and Israelite camps. As darkness fell, the cloud turned to fire, lighting up the night. But the Egyptians

---

[97] 2 Chronicles 20:15b, KJV.
[98] 2 Chronicles 20:17a, KJV.

and Israelites did not approach each other all night. . . .[23] Then the Egyptians—all of Pharaoh's horses, chariots, and charioteers—chased them into the middle of the sea. [24] But just before dawn **the Lord looked down on the Egyptian army from the pillar of fire and cloud**, and he threw their forces into total confusion."[99]

Spoken centuries later, the words of Isaiah the prophet emphasize the same truth of a God Who carefully watches a nation's social-political developments. Social-political degeneration was taking place in the days of Isaiah the prophet. His message addresses the LORD's concern for His oppressed and weary people.

"[27] Why do you say, O Jacob, And speak, O Israel: **'My way is hidden from the Lord, And my just claim is passed over by my God'?** [28] Have you not known? Have you not heard? The everlasting God, the Lord, The Creator of the ends of the earth, Neither faints nor is weary. **His understanding is unsearchable.** [29] He gives power to the weak, And to *those who have* no might He increases strength. [30] Even the youths shall faint and be weary, And the young men shall utterly fall, [31] But those who wait on the Lord Shall renew *their* strength; They shall mount up with wings like eagles, They shall run and not be weary, They shall walk and not faint."[100]

The God of miraculous acts and social deliverance is watching all things. We who long for God to vindicate those oppressed in the nation find ourselves in a season of waiting. We must—and it is good—to wait upon the LORD to intervene in our national affairs. While waiting and praying

---

[99] Exodus 14:19–20, 23–24, NLT, emphases added.
[100] Isaiah 40:27–31, NKJV, emphases added.

for divine judgment and deliverance, we should resolve in our hearts to trust the LORD for the strength to endure until He acts.

The LORD has attuned Himself to compassionately hear the deafening cries of the suffering masses in America, **"How long, O LORD, how long?!"**

> "[1] The Lord is a God who avenges. O God who avenges, shine forth. [2] Rise up, Judge of the earth; pay back to the proud what they deserve. [3] How long, Lord, will the wicked, how long will the wicked be jubilant?"[101]

"Beams of Heaven as I Go" is a great hymn of the Church and answers the prayer of "How long?" with the word, **"Someday."** Its verses speak to the issue of God's providential care and intervention in the lives of His people who contend with oppression. Stanza three and the hymn's chorus are encouraging words for those of us who proactively and patiently struggle, while waging spiritual warfare against social-political oppressive forces. Someday, God will bring a decisive end to our battles.

"Beams of Heaven as I Go" [102]

Verse 3

> *Harder yet may be the fight;*
> *right may often yield to might;*
> *wickedness a while may reign;*
> *Satan's cause may seem to gain.*

---

[101] Psalm 94:1–3, NIV.
[102] Charles Albert Tindley, ca. 1906. *Lyrics on Hymnsite.com* https://www.hymnsite.com/lyrics/umh524.sht

But there's a God that rules above
with hand of power and heart of love;
and if I'm right, he'll fight my battle,
I shall have peace someday.

Chorus

I do not know how long 'twill be,
nor what the future holds for me,
but this I know: if Jesus leads me,
I shall get home someday.

◊ Destructive Intervention Expected

In the burden of this crucial hour, a strong, and studied, personal conviction presses me to communicate this message. In doing so, I am convinced that in the coming days many other genuine believers will see fit to give their full-hearted endorsement to the same. My conviction tells me that **the LORD is poising Himself for a "Red Sea" intervention in the affairs of our nation.**

It is quite theologically tenable to contend that some type of destructive judgment clearly awaits the oppressive and unspiritual oppositionists in America. These are they who persistently pursue an unethical and obstructionist social agenda that attempts to roll back the nation's progress in the areas of freedom and justice. Those who pursue this kind of social-political persecution place themselves in peril; they tempt the LORD to destructively intervene, and they should not be surprised when He does.

Divine intervention of a destructive nature follows on the heels of the marching army who defiantly pursues their

liberated former captives. When the longsuffering of God finally tires of the foolishly perverted ways and high-handed iniquity of social oppressors, the LORD simply overflows His wrath upon the sinful situation. Thus, we should fully expect that the LORD will intervene to end the persecutory politics taking place in America.

Though they differ, a divine judgment has similarities to the law of sowing and reaping. God has designed sowing and reaping as a part of the natural order of things, a process that happens all the time in everyday life. Consider the following.

> "⁷ Don't be misled—you cannot mock the justice of God. You will always harvest what you plant. ⁸ Those who live only to satisfy their own sinful nature will harvest decay and death from that sinful nature. But those who live to please the Spirit will harvest everlasting life from the Spirit."[103]

> "For they have sown the wind, and they shall reap the whirlwind . . ."[104]

> "⁸ In my experience, only those who plant seeds of evil harvest trouble, ⁹ and then they are swept away by the angry breath of God."[105]

Most people normally expect this kind of sowing and reaping. However, the effects of divine punishment exceed the results of normal sowing and reaping. The consequences of receiving a divine judgment are often far more intensified than those received from the natural law of sowing and reaping.

---

[103] Galatians 6:7–8, NLT.
[104] Hosea 8:7a, KJV.
[105] Job 4:8–9, CEV.

For the sake of clarity, **I reiterate the conviction that the defiant political oppressors in our nation are in line to experience a divine judgment.** Owing to their persecutory practices, they stand to experience an affliction that goes beyond reaping the normal adverse results for the sin they have sown. Divine retribution marks them for greater suffering.

In His own sovereign and providential way, I believe that the LORD will permit some form of a terrible and irreparable ruin to come upon the nation's prominent political oppressors. By doing so, God will deliver those who have been suffering political-social affliction from these persecutory leaders. The LORD will deliver the downtrodden from the oppressive political ways of the nation's obstinate tyrannic leaders who otherwise would have continued operating in America's democracy—save for the LORD's destructive intervention.

> "The Lord has a reason for everything he does, and he lets evil people live only to be punished."[106]

How? When?

How near to arrival is God's vindication for the oppressed of America's land? The idea is plausible that a divine intervention may be **imminent**. Or, perhaps, we stand to uncover and discern the nature of its destructive effects that are already in process. In the chaotic and troubling political atmosphere that we are experiencing, could it be that God has already set up the American Ol' Pharaoh and his pursuing army for a devastating "drowning?"

---

[106] Proverbs 16:4, CEV.

Who knows? Only God knows for sure.

In a future that is not too distant, and in His own mysterious way, the Warrior-Deliverer God may choose to decisively act. The LORD may quickly move to overthrow the nation's defiant political oppressors. And He may do so in such an obvious manner that makes it nearly impossible for anyone to deny that the hand of God has directed the spiritual punishment of those who are political persecutors.

Politically oppressive leaders in America should take a warning from the devastating loss of life experienced by the Ol' Pharaoh's army at the Red Sea. When the days of divine intervention and reckoning come, defiant political oppressors will suffer, but not alone. Their families will also suffer divine consequences.

Why is it that many socially oppressive leaders fail to seriously consider how their actions will have repercussions for and negatively impact their immediate family and those they love the most? Many politicians calculate how their decisions and actions will impact their political enemies. But they blind their eyes to the spiritual and wider ramifications of their mean-spirited actions for their close family and community relations.

Consider: How many people are suffering spiritual consequences due to the oppressive practices of their kindred elected or appointed political leaders? Children, spouses, and other relations stand to suffer the loss of a loved one who just would not lead righteously, betrayed the public trust, oppressed and persecuted the people, and thereby incurred a special punishment from God.

Some of the LORD's people are spiritually "ready to roll" with His divine judgment. Faith-obedience has charged their spiritual temperament. These proactivist saints are far past ready to encounter or welcome a life-destroying experience that the LORD has designed to put an end to the oppressive political madness of Trumpism that has pervaded and afflicted our social space.

It is within the sanctified scope of our spiritual temper that we long to see an awe-inspiring divine deliverance for the oppressed and marginalized people of our land. For these acts of God, we spiritually prepare ourselves. By His grace we are ready to stand as truth-telling witnesses who obediently make a confession in the spirit of our faith, **"Amen. The LORD's will be done."**

In doing so we do not avenge ourselves, but rather . . .

". . . [we] give place to wrath; for it is written, **'Vengeance is Mine, I will repay,'** says the Lord."[107]

---

[107] Romans 12:19b, emphasis added, NKJV.

4

Justified Rejoicing
in
Divine Justice

When God sends a judgment upon defiant political oppressors there is an occasion to celebrate and rejoice. Some may take exception to this response by followers of Christ. "Where is your compassion?" they would say. "You shouldn't rejoice when someone has a destructive experience or dies."

It is necessary to address this and related concerns.

Repentance, Forgiveness, and Eternal Destiny

◊ Forgiveness Follows Repentance

Someone may object to the teaching of a divine judgment by saying that a Christian must forgive. There are perhaps millions of Christians in the nation (white Evangelical or otherwise) who have "forgiven" an oppressor for his errant ways. The issue of extending forgiveness raises a crucial question: Is it righteous for a Christian to extend forgiveness to someone who has not asked for forgiveness? Or to one who has not demonstrated a change in behavior that warrants forgiveness by those he has offended?

The very words spoken by Jesus directly address the issue of extending forgiveness to someone who has committed offenses. Jesus' words in the Gospel of Luke are straightforward:

> "[3] So watch yourselves. 'If your brother or sister sins against you, rebuke them; and if they repent, forgive them.'" (Luke 17:3, NIV)

"**If they repent**," Jesus said. "**If**. . ." Based on these words of our Lord, I believe that millions of Christ's followers are in error when they offer forgiveness to an offender who has not repented of their transgression, nor asked for forgiveness. Their zeal for extending forgiveness is good. But over against the clear teaching of our LORD, something has skewed their knowledge of repentance as a prerequisite to seeking or bestowing forgiveness.

We should also note that when Jesus was dying on the cross, He continually prayed that God would forgive His victimizers:

"Jesus said, 'Father, forgive them, for they don't know what they are doing.' And the soldiers gambled for his clothes by throwing dice."[108]

Notice that the Lord in His prayer did not address those who were crucifying them. **He addressed His intercessory prayer to His Father:** "Father, forgive them . . ." were His compassionate words. Not once did the Lord speak directly to the Roman centurions (or to others who sullied their hands with His crucifixion) with the words: "I forgive you for crucifying Me."

Stephen, a servant in the early Church, experienced persecution for following Christ. The biblical story records his death as the first martyr of the Christian faith. When his enemies were stoning Stephen to death, he uttered an intercessory prayer of forgiveness like that of our Lord:

"[59] And they stoned Stephen as he was calling on *God* and saying, "Lord Jesus, receive my spirit." [60] Then he knelt down and cried out with a loud voice, "Lord, do not charge them with this sin." And when he had said this, he fell asleep."[109]

As he was dying, Stephen did not directly speak to his persecutors and say, "I forgive you for stoning me." No. **Instead, Stephen asked the LORD not to place his unjustified death on the account of his murderers**. He commended the matter of their forgiveness into the hands of our sovereign God. Stephen petitioned the LORD to adjudicate the horrendous actions of the persecutors. **God alone would**

---

[108] Luke 23:34, NLT.
[109] Acts 7:59–60, NKJV.

determine whether He would absolve these oppressors of any consequences they should experience for their guilt.

We, as our Lord, should offer forgiveness to those who ask after they show a sign of true repentance. In this way, the Lord forgave the repentant thief who the soldiers were crucifying alongside our Lord.[110] In this way the Lord also completely forgave the sinful woman who silently demonstrated her repentance and petition for His forgiveness by her compassionate actions.[111]

What if a defiant political oppressor claims to be a Christian?

> "[19] But God's truth stands firm like a foundation stone with this inscription: 'The LORD knows those who are his,' and 'All who belong to the LORD must turn away from evil.'"[112]

If an oppressor is a nominal "Christian," then his Christian community should rebuke him for his wrongs.[113] When he repents of those wrongs (not just changes his mind but changes his attitude and actions—true repentance) then his Christian community should forgive him. And then they have the responsibility to require that he make amends to persons—and the nation—for the dirt he has done.

What if an oppressive persecutor is not a Christian? Then the Christian community must leave it to the Lord to judge him as an "outsider" to Christ-centered faith.

---

[110] See Luke 23:39–43.
[111] See Luke 7:36ff., especially verses 48–50.
[112] 2 Timothy 2:19, NLT.
[113] See Luke 17:3–4; and Matthew 18:15ff.

"[12] **It isn't my responsibility to judge outsiders,** but it certainly is your responsibility to judge those inside the church who are sinning. [13] **God will judge those on the outside;** but as the Scriptures say, 'You must remove the evil person from among you.'"[114]

◊ Checking Hypocritical Unrepentance

A good conscience before God, that calls all to be humane and righteous, must check any prideful and self-righteous personality traits in one's life. In the days of Jesus, some persons held a judgmental perspective about the tragic experiences of others. They thought that the persons who lost their lives deserved their fate (divine judgment) because they were greater sinners than others. In this context, Jesus gave a stern warning to those who hypocritically (and therefore incorrectly) analyzed the situation of those who tragically lost their lives.

"[1] About this time Jesus was informed that Pilate had murdered some people from Galilee as they were offering sacrifices at the Temple. [2] 'Do you think those Galileans were worse sinners than all the other people from Galilee?' Jesus asked. 'Is that why they suffered? [3] Not at all! And you will perish, too, unless you repent of your sins and turn to God. [4] And what about the eighteen people who died when the tower in Siloam fell on them? Were they the worst sinners in Jerusalem? [5] No, and I tell you again that unless you repent, you will perish, too.'"[115]

---

[114] 1 Corinthians 5:12–13, NLT, emphases added.
[115] Luke 13:1–5, NLT.

Note that Jesus did not dismiss the idea of a judgment/ punishment that would come upon a sinner, divine or otherwise. Instead, the Lord warned all His listeners to "repent," or to face similar dire consequences/divine judgments. Jesus spoke His words against **hypocritically unrepentant analysts**. Moreover, the critique given by Jesus maintained **a solid connection between judgment and unrepentance**. In this instance, "**Repent or perish**" was His overriding message.

God Himself does not take pleasure in the downfall of persons, even when they receive punishment for their sin.[116] God would rather that sinners repent by taking a different course and averting judgment. Nevertheless, though it hurts His heart, God occasionally sends remedial judgments upon sinners/oppressors for the injustice they show to others.

"[32] Though he brings grief, he also shows compassion because of the greatness of his unfailing love. [33] For he does not enjoy hurting people or causing them sorrow. [34] **If people crush underfoot all the prisoners of the land,** [35] **if they deprive others of their rights in defiance of the Most High,** [36] **if they twist justice in the courts—doesn't the Lord see all these things?** [37] Who can command things to happen without the Lord's permission? [38] Does not the Most High send both calamity and good? [39] **Then why should we, mere humans, complain when we are punished for our sins?** [40] Instead, let us test and examine our ways. Let us turn back to the Lord. [41] Let us lift our hearts and hands to God in heaven and say, [42] 'We have sinned and rebelled, and you have not forgiven us.'"[117]

---

[116] See Lamentations 3:33; Ezekiel 33:11.
[117] Lamentations 3:32–42, NLT, emphases added.

◊ Earthly Judgment, Eternal Destiny

When this discussion speaks about a divine judgment upon political oppressors, it is addressing a divine punishment that a person receives in this life. **This message is not addressing the issue of eternal destiny, i.e., whether an oppressor ends up in hell, and not in heaven.** Understanding the nature of eternal damnation, it would be quite spiritually distasteful to rejoice over someone who has lost their soul for eternity. No, the idea of rejoicing specified here is a rejoicing over the Lord's chastisement of a person's life on this side of eternity.

Based on their personal response to the Lord Jesus, each person chooses their own eternal destiny, and God alone ultimately determines their final state.[118] However, we may seek to discern the eternal path that a person has chosen by observing their attitude, words, and actions. The good ways and beliefs of some persons seem to point to their enjoying an eternal fellowship with God. The bad ways and unbelief of others appear to point to an eternal destiny that separates them from the presence of God.

The Lord Himself knows for certain where each person stands in relationship to eternal salvation. Each person also knows whether within their heart they have the assuring witness, through God's Spirit, of a personal relationship with the LORD their Savior.

"He who believes in the Son of God has the witness in himself;"[119]

---

[118] "For *whoever calls* on the name of the LORD shall be saved'" Romans 10:13, NKJV.

[119] 1 John 5:10a, NKJV. See Romans 8:16.

Sometimes God administers a divine judgment on Earth to a person whose destiny is heaven.

"Then you must throw this man out and hand him over to Satan so **that his sinful nature will be destroyed and he himself will be saved** on the day the Lord returns."[120]

Sometimes seemingly opposite emotions simultaneously pervade the lives of mature believers. Sorrow and rejoicing often come together. It is a valid Christian experience to at once be "sorrowful, yet always rejoicing."[121] Yes, it is possible, and in many instances advisable, for a person to express the full range of their emotions in response to a destructive judgment or a preserving deliverance from God.

We feel sorrow because a person has died. Yet, we rejoice because the evil-inclined person is gone; God has moved them out of the way. And when the justice of God has moved an evil-minded social-political troublemaker out of the way, the meek and lowly of the Earth—the ones who suffer most from oppression—are able to breathe a little easier. Genuine believers rejoice with those whom God delivers; with those who find themselves encircled by divine protection.

Love, Justice, and Truth

What place has rejoicing with love, justice, and truth?

Showing true love and seeking equitable justice are two sides of one coin. They go together. Because we love those who are captives and oppressed, we seek justice for them

---

[120] 1 Corinthians 5:5, NLT, emphasis added. See also 1 Corinthians 11:30–32; contrast Acts 13:6–12.

[121] 2 Corinthians 6:10, KJV.

by resisting and working against the oppressive forces that control them. We hate the attitudes and acts of oppressors. Yet, we extend love to those who must quit their oppressive practices. We seek to save them from the self-destroying snares of the injustice they perpetrate.

However, most oppressors do not allow others to love them in a way of truth. **Oppressors reject truth.** In contrast, most of those who suffer oppression will receive the true love that compassionate persons express. **True love is just love.**

Truth and love are twins: they must live and work together, especially in pursuit of "the beloved community."

> "[1] This letter is from John, the elder. I am writing to the chosen lady and to her children, **whom I love in the truth**—as does everyone else who knows the truth—[2] because the truth lives in us and will be with us forever."[122]

We must not forget the words written in 1 Corinthians 13, the love chapter in the Scripture. In verse 6 we read:

> "[Love] does not rejoice at injustice *and* unrighteousness, but rejoices when right *and* truth prevail."[123]

The redemptive love of God rejoices when righteousness and truth prevail over lawlessness, injustice, and lies. **Love rejoices when a divine judgment becomes the remedy for deception, wickedness, and evil.**

A community of genuine love that would protect the least

---

[122] 2 John 1–2, NLT, emphasis added. See also 2 John 3, and 3 John 1.
[123] 1 Corinthians 13:5–6, ANT.

in our society, while seeking to redeem its oppositionists, is based on truth and its reliable information. It is not based on the 25,000+ lies, deceptions, falsehoods, misleading claims, attacks on so-called "fake news," and the like that characterize the discordant relationship the oppressive ex-president has with truth and related facts. Otherwise, without truth there is no foundation for building authentic community.

We should rejoice in the sought-after outcomes.

Millions in the nation rejoiced greatly when the new president defeated the incumbent. We rejoiced that God used our votes to elect a new leader freely and fairly. We were thankful for the outcome. Likewise, **it is right to rejoice when God uses divine judgment to move a defiant oppressor out of the way**.

Apart from human actions, God may decisively bring justice and freedom to misused and abused people. When God does His thing in His own way, our rejoicing and praise should intensify. We must praise God whether we attribute the divine outcome to our votes or to direct intervention by God. God gives us the privilege (and we have a responsibility) to thank and praise God for all the liberating outcomes for which we have earnestly prayed, and that God has decisively answered.

Rejoicing in *Revelation* and a Song of Celebration

◊ Rejoicing in *Revelation*

The book of Revelation presents the idea of rejoicing when those who are God's enemies receive a divine judgment. Consider the following:

- **When the forces of God
throw the dragon down from heaven:**

"[10] Then I heard a loud voice shouting across the heavens, **'It has come at last— salvation and power and the Kingdom of our God, and the authority of his Christ.** For the accuser of our brothers and sisters has been thrown down to earth— the one who accuses them before our God day and night. [11] And they have defeated him by the blood of the Lamb and by their testimony. And they did not love their lives so much that they were afraid to die. [12] Therefore, rejoice, O heavens! And you who live in the heavens, rejoice! But terror will come on the earth and the sea, for the devil has come down to you in great anger, knowing that he has little time.'"[124]

- **When Babylon falls:**

"**Rejoice over her fate**, O heaven and people of God and apostles and prophets! For at last God has judged her for your sakes."[125]

"[1] After this, I heard what sounded like a vast crowd in heaven shouting, **'Praise the Lord!** Salvation and glory and power belong to our God. [2] His judgments are true and just. **He has punished the great prostitute** who corrupted the earth with her immorality. He has avenged the murder of his servants.' [3] And again their voices rang out: **'Praise the Lord! The smoke from that city ascends forever and ever!'**"[126]

---

[124] Revelation 12:10–12, NLT, emphasis added.
[125] Revelation 18:20, NLT, emphasis added.
[126] Revelation 19:1–3, NLT, emphases added.

◊ **Reciting a Song of Celebration—
Exodus 15:1–21**

God's wisdom has included Exodus 15:1–21 in His sacred Word. It is the victory song of Moses, Miriam, and the delivered Israelites. This celebratory song was composed and sung directly in response to the LORD's judgment on Ol' Pharaoh's army, and His deliverance of the Israelites at the Red Sea. This is the people's song of praise for the victory that the LORD gave to them over their enemies.

It was appropriate for the Israelites to rejoice in the LORD their God for defeating Ol' Pharaoh and his pursuing army. It is likewise commendable for believers to rejoice when God defeats our defiant oppressors in the "Red Sea" experiences that we encounter. We must praise the LORD when He gives us a miraculous victory over our formidable foes.

In our rejoicing we encourage those who rejoice to praise God in the actual words of Exodus 15. The Scripture reads:

"Then Moses and the people of Israel sang this song to the Lord..."[127]

Here are some of those words of praise:

"'[1b] I will sing to the Lord, for he has triumphed gloriously; he has hurled both horse and rider into the sea. [2] The Lord is my strength and my song; he has given me victory. This is my God, and I will praise him— my father's God, and I will exalt him! [3] The Lord is a warrior; Yahweh is his name! [4] Pharaoh's chariots and army he

---
[127] Exodus 15:1a, NLT.

has hurled into the sea. The finest of Pharaoh's officers are drowned in the Red Sea. ⁵ The deep waters gushed over them; they sank to the bottom like a stone. ⁶ 'Your right hand, O Lord, is glorious in power. Your right hand, O Lord, smashes the enemy. ⁷ In the greatness of your majesty, you overthrow those who rise against you. You unleash your blazing fury; it consumes them like straw. . . .¹¹ 'Who is like you among the gods, O Lord—glorious in holiness, awesome in splendor, performing great wonders? ¹² You raised your right hand, and the earth swallowed our enemies. ¹³ "With your unfailing love you lead the people you have redeemed. In your might, you guide them to your sacred home. . . .¹⁸ The Lord will reign forever and ever!'. . . .

²¹ And Miriam sang this song:

'Sing to the Lord, for he has triumphed gloriously; he has hurled both horse and rider into the sea.' "¹²⁸

---

¹²⁸ Exodus 15:1b–7, 11–13, 18, 21, NLT, emphasis added.

5

WATCHPERSONS FOR THE NATION

A Pivotal Hour

Most of those who analyze the painful times besetting the nation are convinced that America is yet at a pivotal hour in the nation's history. The political developments and social repercussions are just that serious. In times like these, genuine followers of Jesus Christ have a responsibility to watch and pray . . . and to serve as watchpersons on the walls of the nation. We must always have a truthful and pertinent answer for those who ask,

> "Watchman, how much longer until morning? When will the night be over?"[129]

Preparing our people for a type of "Red Sea" destructive/deliverance intervention is in order. It is better than not to prepare for the eventuality of a divine breakthrough that makes a significantly positive political impact—one that helps the least of these and uplifts those who are downtrodden. True followers of Christ Jesus are not beyond theological reasonableness to **expect such an overflowing movement from God in His own time—if the political and social oppressors refuse to quit**.

In this season of political, health, economic, and racial uncertainties, during this night of the nation's current crises, we are wise to stay alert and take heed. All people of faith-obedience should position one another to anticipate a spiritual manifestation of great national magnitude—even of a judgment/deliverance by the outstretched mighty arm of the LORD.

A Reprieve?

Has there been a delay in a divine judgment? Or could the persecutors avert a God-directed punishment? Possibly.

Many of us expected that the outcome of the presidential election would help to sufficiently settle, at the least, the nation's immediate and pressing political turbulence. The prospect of having a new Biden administration has led many to believe that this significant change in leadership will

---

[129] Isaiah 21:11b, NLT, emphasis added.

help to turn the country around for the better. However, there is a word of caution to convey.

Despite the promise of progress by the new administration, the hopes of many in America may begin to fade, even as they seek to cope with the aftermath of life-altering events that continue to adversely impact their living and progress.[130] The effects of national crises continue a daily onslaught on our lives. COVID-19 continues to rage. In some sectors there is a growing uneasiness about whether the new administration can effectively govern a very divided nation, sufficiently enough to correct its mounting problems. Ex-president Trump and the ideological adherents of Trumpism remain a hostile and potent thorn in the side of the nation. Early indicators suggest that their political opposition against the new president is ongoing and increasing, **if not entrenching**.

It is certain that the new president must continue to act decisively and quickly, for the window of opportunity for making sweeping changes will not stay open long. Whereas the ex-president sought to illegitimately overturn the freedom-work of God, the new president must reverse the course. President Biden and Vice President Harris must seek to further the freedoms, justice, and truth that thrust them into office, as the trajectory of the election's outcome demonstrated. Their utmost responsibility is to **continue**

---

[130] On day one, President Biden issued a number of executive actions to combat pressing national issues. These included the coronavirus, climate change, inequality and racism, democracy, truth, and America's role in the world. See David Leonhardt, "Cascading Crises of our Era: The Biden administration begins to address the six crises that the new president described in his inaugural address," *The New York Times,* Jan. 21, 2021. https://www.nytimes.com/2021/01/21/briefing/executive-orders-biden-climate-proud-boys.html

the righteous path of showing mercy to the poor, a divinely-sanctioned mandate for those who govern.

> "[27] Therefore, O king, let my advice be acceptable to you; break off your sins by *being* **righteous**, and your iniquities by **showing mercy to the poor.** Perhaps there may be a lengthening of your prosperity. . . . [32b]know that the **Most High rules in the kingdom of men, and gives it to whomever He chooses.**"[131]

Jesus proclaimed these social-political words of Jubilee:

> "[18] 'The Spirit of the Lord is upon Me, Because He has anointed Me **To gospelize the poor.** He has sent Me to heal the brokenhearted, To proclaim liberty to the captives And recovery of sight to the blind, To set at liberty those who are oppressed; [19] To proclaim the acceptable year of the Lord.'"[132]

Jesus also taught this political truth:

> "Render therefore to Caesar the things that are Caesar's, and to God the things that are God's."[133]

Though one primary goal of the president is to counter-act the national political divide by working for unity across the aisle, his administration must stay focused on liberating the oppressed and preserving their freedoms. He must not compromise the truth, justice, and freedom agenda by bending over backward to work with those who come from

---

[131] Daniel 4:27, 32b, NKJV, emphases added.
[132] Luke 4:18–19, NKJV, literal emphasis added.
[133] Luke 20:25b, NKJV.

opposing camps, some of whom have gone on record as supporters of "The Big Lie" of a stolen election, or as allies of the insurrectionists.[134] Otherwise, in his quest to unite the nation, Biden may unintentionally acquiesce to perpetuating the oppressions and persecutions of those whom God was setting free through the historic election.

The presidential election has demonstrated that God clearly spoke and enacted a change toward truth, justice, and freedom through the voting voice of the American populace—a change that Ol' Pharaoh and his army should support, or at least acknowledge as true. **Perhaps they may avert divine judgment.**

A Warning

In no uncertain terms, **Trumpism ideologues should unequivocally desist from pursuing their contrary and hostile socio-political—and obviously ungodly—agenda.** Herein we warn all these defiant political oppressors not to take the longsuffering patience of the LORD for granted. Neither by their wrongdoing should they continue to arrogantly tempt His wrath. It is extremely dangerous for America's Ol' Pharaoh and his army to keep pursuing a subversive agenda and demonic stratagem against the freedom-work of God.

---

[134] See, Catie Edmondson and Luke Broadwater, "Before Capitol Riot, Republican Lawmakers Fanned the Flames," *The New York Times,* Jan. 11, 2021. Updated Jan. 13, 2021. https://www.ny-times.com/2021/01/11/us/politics/republicans-capitol-riot.html See, Karen Yourish, Larry Buchanan and Denise Lu, "The 147 Republicans Who Voted to Overturn Election Results," *The New York Times.* Updated Jan. 7, 2021. https://www.nytimes.com/interactive/2021/01/07/us/elections/electoral-college-biden-ob-jectors.html

By continuing to do so, they surely draw themselves ever so close to facing God-driven dire and remedial spiritual consequences.

Historically and theologically based foresight insightfully warns us that a Divine intervention should be coming. It is only a matter of time. Past judgments and deliverances of God point to similar actions that He may see fit to perform in our present circumstances.

Be ever mindful: the effects of a divine judgment **will always supersede** personal progress or social-political gains. Receiving punishment from the hands of the Warrior-Deliverer God is no joke. Nothing is fake about the terrifying retribution of an angered God.

> "[30] For we know the one who said, 'I will take revenge. I will pay them back.' He also said, 'The Lord will judge his own people.' [31] **It is a terrible thing to fall into the hands of the living God.**"[135]

Peace.

[135] Hebrews 10:30–31, NLT, emphasis added.

Small Books Big Ideas is an imprint of Black Light Fellowship, and is the collaborative brainchild of Mary C. Lewis, MCL Editing, Etc., and the publisher. Michelle D. Muhammad, of MDM Design created the logo for SBBI.

The concept of **Small Books Big Ideas** is simple: while the book's size/number of pages is **small**, the ideas embedded are "**big**." The SBBI imprint emphasizes the following:

- Communicating to those demanding societal change;
- Understanding resistance to change, and equipping persons and organizations with the knowledge they need to expand awareness about resistance;
- Increasing potential to forgive/(re)unite; and
- Responding to questions about the holistic health of individuals, families, churches, and communities.

SBBI launches in Spring 2021. Its initial publication is *Defiant Political Oppressors Invite a Divine Judgment.*

Contact Information

Rev. Dr. Walter Arthur McCray

Office Phone: 773-826-7790

Website: https://www.BlackLightFellowship.com

NBEA Website: http://www.The-NBEA.org

Email: info@blacklightfellowship.com